SPEECHSONG

BEFORE YOU START TO READ THIS BOOK, take this moment to think about making a donation to punctum books, an independent non-profit press,

@ https://punctumbooks.com/support/

If you're reading the e-book, you can click on the image below to go directly to our donations site. Any amount, no matter the size, is appreciated and will help us to keep our ship of fools afloat. Contributions from dedicated readers will also help us to keep our commons open and to cultivate new work that can't find a welcoming port elsewhere. Our adventure is not possible without your support.

Vive la Open Access.

Fig. 1. Hieronymus Bosch, *Ship of Fools* (1490–1500)

SPEECHSONG: THE GOULD/SCHOENBERG DIALOGUES. Copyright © 2020 by Richard Cavell. This work carries a Creative Commons BY-NC-SA 4.0 International license, which means that you are free to copy and redistribute the material in any medium or format, and you may also remix, transform and build upon the material, as long as you clearly attribute the work to the authors (but not in a way that suggests the authors or punctum books endorses you and your work), you do not use this work for commercial gain in any form whatsoever, and that for any remixing and transformation, you distribute your rebuild under the same license. http://creativecommons.org/licenses/by-nc-sa/4.0/

First published in 2020 by punctum books, Earth, Milky Way.
https://punctumbooks.com

ISBN-13: 978-1-950192-49-6 (print)
ISBN-13: 978-1-950192-50-2 (ePDF)

DOI: 10.21983/P3.0267.1.00

LCCN: 2019951804
Library of Congress Cataloging Data is available from the Library of Congress

Book design: Vincent W.J. van Gerven Oei
Cover image: Stephen Prina, *A Structural Analysis and Reconstruction of MS7098 as Determined by the Difference Between the Measurements of Duration and Displacement* (1990); 12 inch Phonograph record with insert poster, 1980; Available at the Music Box, $8.99; Design program, 1984 (poster, merchandising display, and publicity photograph); Reconstituted arrangement, 1990 (pressed vinyl, offset lithography on paper, gelatin silver print on masonite, gelatin silver print, integrated amplifier, turntable, headphones, table, two chairs, lacquer-rubbed maple). Courtesy of the artist and of Petzel, New York.

HIC SVNT MONSTRA

Richard Cavell

SPEECHSONG
The Gould/Schoenberg Dialogues

Contents

Introduction   13

Speechsong

Act One   23
Act Two   31
Sources   39

Glenn Gould and Arnold Schoenberg: *quasi parlando*

one   47
two   55
three   59
four   67
five   77
six   81
seven   87
eight   95
nine   103
ten   107
eleven   113
twelve   125

Bibliography   137

Acknowledgments

As an avid listener to the Canadian Broadcasting Corporation's radio programming in the 1960s, my first encounter with Glenn Gould was through his sound documentaries. I had no idea then that he shared his media interests with his Toronto neighbor and mentor, Marshall McLuhan, but that nexus became a focus of my first book, as I learned about their mutual interest in acoustic space. And when *The Glenn Gould Reader* was published in 1984, the importance of Arnold Schoenberg to Gould was emphatically declared. I am fortunate to be a researcher at a university that houses a vibrant music school; Richard Kurth and David Metzer encouraged me along the way to *Speechsong*, and Doreen Oke instructed me in the intricacies of the baroque keyboard, which gave me further insights into the complexities of Gould's and Schoenberg's practices. Conversations with Raviv Ganchrow, Professor in the Institute of Sonology (The Hague), attuned me to the complexities of the sonic environment. The Petzel Gallery, New York, generously allowed me to use Stephen Prina's compelling image for the book cover. Vincent W.J. van Gerven Oei, my publisher and editor, was a pleasure to work with; he must really be a consortium of ten people, and I thank them all. *Speechsong* could not have been written without the support of Peter Dickinson. I dedicate this book to him.

Introduction

Glenn Gould (1932–1982) and Arnold Schoenberg (1874–1951) present themselves to us as enigmas. Schoenberg is one of the most influential composers of the 20th century, yet his work is rarely heard in concert. Gould — one of Schoenberg's most prolific commentators — is among the greatest pianists of the 20th century, yet he recused himself from the concert hall at the height of his career and spent the rest of his life in the recording studio. These paradoxes have given rise to an immense critical legacy. Musicological studies of Schoenberg, however, have tended to focus on him as a musical theorist rather than composer, and critical studies of Gould have tended to construct him as an eccentric pianist whose embrace of the recording studio was in pursuit of perfection.

Speechsong addresses these paradoxes orthogonally. As a critical performance text that works both inside and outside established generic frameworks of performance work and critical study, *Speechsong* argues that the interface between speaking and singing that Schoenberg created in *Sprechgesang* opens his work and that of Gould to an analysis based on the notion of mediation. Attention to media is able to foreground the cultural importance of Schoenberg as having produced an understanding of acoustic space as the contemporary environment in which we experience performance. A similar argument can be made for Gould, who likewise articulated a new soundscape through his radio documentaries and his acoustic orchestrations. Both Schoenberg and Gould find their contemporary place not in "music" *per se,* nor in the concert hall, but on YouTube and in practices such as composed theater, post-internet art, and sound installations.

Speechsong is structured in two parts. The first part draws on the practice of composed theater to imagine an on-stage dialogue between Schoenberg and Gould. The conversation takes place in the Wilshire Ebell Theater, Los Angeles, where Schoenberg's compositions were often performed during his Californian exile, and where Gould gave his last public performance in April 1964. The two parts of the dialogue are structured to reflect Schoenberg's *magnum opus,* the opera *Moses und Aron,* in order to reframe questions raised in the opera about art and mediation. These questions are considered at length in the second half of the book, an essay in twelve "moments" titled "Glenn Gould and Arnold Schoenberg — *quasi parlando.*"

At bottom Glenn played only the Goldberg Variations *and the* Art of the Fugue, *even when he was playing other pieces, such as by Brahms and Mozart, or Schönberg and Webern; he held the latter two in the highest regard, but he placed Schönberg above Webern, not the other way around, as people claim.*

— Thomas Bernhard, *The Loser*

Most composers know nothing of Schoenberg's approach to painting nor do most painters know much about his style of composition. The pianist had seen most of the self-portraits, yet had never before seen the *Blue Self-Portrait,* so stopped before that blue, felt the anxiety and chill, the awareness of time and negative space folding into itself, sought some affirmation that he knew would be pointless, bent over the case that held Schoenberg's letter. He had peered at the letter and read it three or four times from the bottom up, starting with the signature which he knew and recognized, it was a humdrum letter to the Reich's culture minister, Schoenberg pleading with the culture minister to recognize his music's value to the nation, imploring one last time but too late, had in reality already said fuck off to the Nazis, fuck off face-to-face, Scheisse! Schoenberg's face versus the Nazi's face — that Schoenberg had balls the pianist reflected as indeed he did every time he thought about Schoenberg, thought to himself while standing there facing the Blue Self-Portrait, to have balls or not to have them, the blue's affront to the radiant sky and its chortling countryside, Scheisse to the Nazis long before they were marching through Munich.

— Noémi Lefebvre, *Blue Self-Portrait*

Ah Dr. Mann [...] [y]ou wrote *the* novel of music, *Faustus,* everyone agrees about that, except poor Schoenberg who, they say, was very jealous about it. Ah, those musicians. Never content. Huge egos. You say that Schoenberg is Nietzsche plus Mahler, an inimitable genius, and he complains. He complains that you called him Adrian Leverkühn and not Arnold Schoenberg, probably. Maybe he'd have been very happy that you devoted six hundred pages of a novel to him, four years of your genius, calling him by his name, Schoenberg, even though when it comes down to it, it wasn't him, but a Nietzsche who reads Adorno [...].
— Mathias Énard, *Compass*

I went inside the store. The pianist, Glenn Gould, appeared on a flatscreen: he and Yehudi Menuhin were performing the Bach sonata I had recognized. There was Glenn Gould hunched over the piano, wearing a dark suit, hearing patterns far beyond the range of what most of us are given to perceive…
— Madeleine Thien, *Do Not Say We Have Nothing*

For as well the pillar of cloud, as that of fire, did the office of directing.
— John Donne, *Essayes in Divinity*

SPEECHSONG

Act One

The performance text is a staged dialogue between a young Glenn Gould and a ghostly Arnold Schoenberg on the occasion of Gould's retirement from the concert hall. The piece is structured according to the dynamics of Schoenberg's (unfinished) opera *Moses und Aron,* in which the divinely inspired Moses finds that words fail to convey his vision, and so must speak through his brother Aron. In the opera, Moses communicates through speechsong (*Sprechstimme* or *Sprechgesang*), a confluence of singing and speaking that is neither one nor the other. Aron sings.

Before the curtain goes up, we hear Schoenberg's *String Quartet no. 2* (op. 10), version for string orchestra and soprano, which has been playing while the audience is still in the lobby. As the curtain goes up (lights down) we hear the piece about 2 minutes before the soprano begins singing (in the 4th movement). When she begins, lights slowly come up so that after a moment we can see Gould and Schoenberg. They are dressed for performance: black suits and white ties. Each is seated at a grand piano, facing each other. The lid of Gould's piano is up; that of Schoenberg's piano is down. Schoenberg speaks with a heavy Viennese accent, and Gould in the clipped voice familiar from his radio broadcasts. The scene is the Wilshire Ebell Theater in

Los Angeles. A large photographic portrait of Schoenberg hangs on the wall at the rear of the stage. The date is April 10, 1964.

[*AS's* String Quartet no. 2 *(op. 10) is playing at the point (in the fourth movement) where the soprano begins singing the words of the Stefan George poem. This will remain in the background continuously such that it extends to GG's recitation of four lines from the George poem. Fade-out will coincide with the end of the quartet; some looping may be required to achieve this effect*]

GG that passage is so beautiful…
AS in Vienna they shouted at her to stop singing!
GG but you gave new life to music with this piece!
AS they said I killed it
GG to give us something greater
AS that no one was interested in listening to
GG you influenced scores of composers — Boulez, Nono, Babbitt, Cage — and you were lionized when you moved to Los Angeles — Hollywood summoned you to write movie scores!
AS I demanded $50,000 from Irving Thalberg and veto rights. If I was going to commit suicide, I wanted to do it in style
GG you refused to abandon your principles
AS while wondering who I was
GG you are an icon of modern music
AS my music is *not* modern; it is just played badly!
GG you are a composer and theoretician
AS Ravel said my music sounded like it came from a laboratory
GG you composed in response to tonality — to the expectations it arouses
AS forward and backward
GG to the space it demanded
AS to the *Liebestod*
GG to Wagner's move from harmonic parts to the musical whole
AS to Wagner's tonal…complications
GG made possible by the disorder at the heart of his music

AS I wandered from the home key
GG in *Verklärte Nacht*
AS they called it "a calf with six feet"
GG then you expanded the dissonant elements until they couldn't possibly be resolved tonally
AS Strauss said I would have been better off shoveling snow!
GG dissonance for the sake of dissonance?
AS I wrote a book on harmony
GG harmony exists only in repose
AS but music is movement
GG and thus music is dissonance
AS *genau!*
GG it is permitted by modulation
AS which is also ambiguity
GG and expression
AS *Lebensgefühl*
GG a feeling for life
AS nature is beautiful even when we do not understand her
GG …the soprano in the String Quartet…
AS she is singing a poem by Stefan George
GG "I feel air of other planets blowing…
　　I am dissolved in tones…
　　I am only a flicker of the sacred fire;
　　I am only a mumbling of the sacred voice"

[*the music from the string quartet will fade out after this point, with complete fade-out coinciding with the end of the quartet itself*]

AS Mahler had just left for America
GG you lost one of your most important supporters
AS and I lost my wife to Gerstl; then he killed himself a few weeks later
GG when the quartet premiered
AS I dedicated it to my wife
GG even though she abandoned you?
AS she abandoned someone she thought I was

GG like you abandoned tonality?

[*fade-in — faintly — of Gould playing the* Three Piano Pieces *(op. 11), followed by the* Five Piano Pieces *(op. 23) which must continue through the dialogue about Bach*]

AS *alles rückgängig zu machen*
GG trying to reverse everything
AS all achievements had to be overturned
GG your pieces became shorter and shorter
AS they were explorations in depth
GG an escape hatch for the stowaways on the good ship post-Wagnerian
AS we wanted freedom
GG then you fell silent for a decade
AS I was perfecting my solitude
GG Europe was engulfed in war
AS I was seeking
GG for a way to organize chaos
AS *genau!*
GG and the tone row?
AS the tone row would not be part of the work
GG it would not be present in the musical composition?
AS it would stand aloof
GG a present absence
AS as in my paintings

[*projection of Schoenberg's painting* Red Gaze *gradually comes into view on the screen where the Schoenberg portrait was projected*]

GG those portraits haunt me
AS the dissolution of the self
GG a becoming other
AS [*after pause*] Gerstl taught me to paint
GG [*after pause*] you composed spatially
AS vertically and horizontally — in two notes

GG whose themes the listener could not anticipate. This was Adorno's thesis — that your music was a purely formal working-out of the *Zeitgeist* — the compulsion to purge music of everything preconceived, and go beyond the depiction of human emotions — pure, unadulterated expression, with no pre-classical gestures.
AS Adorno was wrong!
GG wrong?
AS the twelve tones were a means, not an end
GG yet your music marks a historical shift
AS a shift toward sound
GG pure chromaticism
AS Thomas Mann thought it was madness
GG *Doctor Faustus*
AS I never forgave Mann for that novel — Leverkühn, he called me — a syphilitic!
GG but surely no one believed him
AS I told a colleague it was absolutely not true
GG and what did they say?
AS they said it was lucky I was shouting in German because the market was rather full …
GG but you threatened to sue Mann
AS he acknowledged that the twelve-tone scale was the work of the "contemporary" [*said disdainfully*] composer Arnold Schoenberg
GG did that please you?
AS I told him that in 20 years we should see who was the "contemporary" of whom!
GG you were always fascinated by numbers!
AS that was the beauty of the 12 tones
GG because …
AS …because the Temple had 12 singers
GG and *Moses und Aron* has 12 letters
AS because I removed an "A" from Aaron's name
GG superstition?
AS belief
GG what did you believe in?

AS my calling as a composer
GG to disrupt the musical past?
AS I was a traditionalist
GG but your twelve tones are radical
AS another kind of freedom
GG like Bach's counterpoint
AS did that draw you to my music?
GG yes; it was the most sustained elaboration of musical mathematics before the Moog synthesizer. I loved the way the first phrase in your *Piano Sonata* breaks down into two easily definable motives of 3 tones each, of which the second is an extension of the first. Then, between tones 2, 3, and 4, and again between 3, 4, and 5, you inserted two other interval groups which bear mathematical correspondence to each other. In both groups the first interval has exactly half the span of the second, while tones 3, 4, and 5 together constitute an augmented inversion of tones 2, 3, 4. In the alto appear two regressive versions of tones 2 to 4, the second in inversion, and the bass proclaims an inverted retrogression of tones 3 to 5, while the tenor goes all the way with an augmentation of tones 3 to 5. Absolutely exhilarating!
AS a *Spiegelbild*
GG a new world of sound
AS from which I constantly deviated
GG this is what electronic technology offered me
AS deviation?
GG The electronic age has forever changed the values that we attach to art. The vocabulary of aesthetic criteria that has been developed since the Renaissance is most concerned with terms that are proving to have little validity for the examination of electronic culture, terms such as "imitation," "invention," and "originality." All of these terms simply serve a crude notion of "progressivism." No work of art is truly original; if it were, it would be unrecognizable. The roles of composer and performer have been combined, and the audiophile listener can now manipulate recordings in such a way as to become their co-producers.

AS a music that is purely music
GG logical and clear
AS sensual and mystic
GG a mystery of communication in a form equally mysterious
AS *Moses und Aron*
GG speechsong
AS ever-unseen
GG oracular
AS immanent
GG inconceivable
AS inexpressible
GG there is only mediation
AS Moses speaks his song
GG Aron sings his speech
AS we must serve a new god

[*lights begin to go down slowly as we hear last notes from op. 23, which should fade out within 60 seconds. During these 60 seconds, GG leaves the stage, then AS, with the music still playing, then fadeout and lights up*]

[INTERLUDE]

[*during the Interlude AS's* Concerto for Piano and Orchestra *(op. 42) is heard in the lobby. The audience may stay in their seats or move into the lobby. Act Two will be announced by the playing of the Bach partita*]

Act Two

[*before lights come up: a projection on the overhead screen of Gould's fingers playing Bach's* Partita no. 6 in E minor *(BWV 830). Lights up, with Gould playing at piano, AS listening. Begin fade when audience seated*]

AS Gould
GG [*stops playing; projection fades*] yes, Master
AS Gould
GG Master?
AS what sort of a name is Gould?
GG [after a pause] it was…Gold
AS Gold?
GG Gold. But my father started spelling it Gould
AS why?
GG because in Toronto in the 1940s it was…difficult…to be Jewish
AS you talk to *me* about difficult!
GG it was difficult because we weren't Jewish
AS not Jewish?
GG we were Jewish during the war
AS I became Jewish again before the war
GG you wanted to restore the Hapsburgs
AS I named my pet rabbit Franz Josef

GG but you were asked to leave the resort at Mattsee
AS because I was Jewish
GG then Kandinsky invited you to join the Bauhaus
AS even Kandinsky was anti-Jewish
GG but he was your friend!
AS I thanked him for making an exception

[*begin fade-in of Schoenberg's* Variations for Orchestra *(op. 31). On the screen, Schoenberg's* Blue Self-Portrait *slowly comes into view*]

GG is that what brought you to Los Angeles?
AS that…and Hitler
GG an escape from history?
AS I tried to interest colleagues in a United Jewish Party and a national homeland
GG did you have any success?
AS no one was interested
GG so you abandoned the West
AS Webern and Berg thought my music was completely Germanic!
GG but America meant safety
AS Los Angeles
GG the west beyond the West
AS Mann called it a flight from cultural crisis
GG it was a flight *to*, not a flight *from*
AS a compromise
GG [*pause*] I just gave my last concert
AS last?
GG I find concertizing degrading
AS what would you rather be doing?
GG making recordings
AS but what about an audience?
GG my recordings reach a much larger audience
AS without the seduction of the concert hall
GG a well-upholstered extension of the Roman Colosseum
AS *genau!*

GG the ear versus the eye gave the listener freedom from the bondage of the concert hall. Recordings do the same, and give the listener what is absolutely unavailable in the concert hall: analytic clarity, immediacy, tactile proximity. The natural home for the symphony is the cavernously ornate concert hall, but your music is music for electronic performance. The *Musikverein* might still be the place to hear music in Vienna, but surely you noticed that in Los Angeles even the doorbells have started ringing in twelve-tone. When you left Europe you left a culture that encountered music in the concert hall and discovered a culture for whom music was synonymous with recording. Hollywood taught you the value of the cut, as opposed to the dissolve. The concert hall is a great place for a Brünnhilde who can surmount without struggle the velvet diapason of the Wagnerian orchestra, but not exactly the venue to trace the filigreed path of the cello in the Dvořák concerto. And recordings have had a huge historical influence — we are the first people who have access to the entire history of musical production, including and especially your beloved Bach.

AS a longing to return to the older style was always vigorous in me

GG Bach is ever new! The Goldbergs were an offshoot of that *Hausmusik* tradition that recordings triumphantly revived, with their contrapuntal extravaganzas, their antiphonal balances, their espousal of instruments that chuff and wheeze and speak directly to a microphone. They were quite simply made for stereo. What Bach taught us in *The Art of the Fugue* is that music is less a matter of creation than of re-creation, the re-assembling of what is already present in the musical system, and this has been fully realized in the recording studio. The stopwatch and tape splice have replaced the opera cape and temper tantrums.

AS conceptual?

[*fade-out of op. 31 at the beginning of this speech and begin fade-in of AS,* Fourth String Quartet *(op. 37) toward its end. This must last through speech about "notation and orchestration," then fade-out]*

GG music became conceptual through recordings — and it became pluralistic. Composer, producer, and tape editor began to merge with the performer, putting an end to the specialism with which tonal music was involved. You were among the first to grasp how recording would change the entire musical process. You realized that the clear sonorities of recording meant that it would be possible to write less heavily instrumented pieces and still achieve maximal effects. This allowed you to attribute significance to minute musical connections and to deal with their subsurface relationships that are best experienced when reproduced electronically. And as this form of performance extends further and further into our private domains, music becomes more and more a part of our lives. And as it does so, it ceases to be art and becomes environmental. In the best of all possible worlds, art would in fact be unnecessary. The audience would be the artist and their lives would be art.

AS transcendence?

GG music is a flow of information. I have always understood my role as making that information say something. But art is not technology. The difference between a Richard Strauss and a Karlheinz Stockhausen is not comparable to the difference between an adding machine and a computer. In fact, in Strauss, the whole process of historical evolution is defied, as are the effete preoccupations of the chronologist. Strauss made his own time richer by not being part of it. He made an argument for individuality, and for his own synthesis of time. Even you found it difficult to fulfil the rhythmic extenuations of your own motivic theories.

AS I returned to Bach

GG like your beloved Brahms

AS Strauss asked if I was a Brahmsian or a Wagnerian; I told him I was a Selfian

GG everything you have written has a resemblance to yourself

AS unlike Stravinsky
GG whose Bach was mere pastiche
AS Modernsky!
GG you satirized him in a piece that sounded the same when the score was read upside down!
AS *genau!*
GG and technique…?
AS …I found technique easy
GG but your music was difficult
AS I refused to harmonize with the old gods
GG "the devil in music"
AS I emancipated the dissonance
GG because home is the journey
AS as it was for Pierrot
GG because no tone is more important than another
AS Wagner called it synagogue noise
GG really?
AS "chant mumbling," he said; "burbling and babbling"
GG yet I've always believed that speech is a form of music. I produced a number of radio documentaries in musical form — rondos, sonatas. Rhythm, texture, tone, dynamics, pacing, and the use of silence were all important to me in these scores. For me, the spoken word was the stuff of music, a form of singing. That's why I sing on my recordings.
AS once, we all sang
GG we fell into speech. Music tries to take us back to song. It's a bridge to another way of being, a relationship between the material and the immaterial, between noise and meaning, medium and message. This is your greatest achievement — greater than any single work: you gave us a new acoustic environment, a new way of listening. Your music sought to recapture the vocalization of Hebrew, a language that sang, a language that can only be sung. And what it sang about was freedom. The *Odyssey* sung by Homer came down to us in thousands of variations, but we do not dare to change one letter of written text. Your music gave us the

freedom to listen again, to listen to speech as it was going over into song.
AS *Sprechgesang*
GG speechsong
AS *genau!*
GG your *Phantasy* is a rhapsodic speech for violin, and in your fourth string quartet the long unison of four instruments in the third movement suggests a vocal line trying to break into utterance
AS "O word that I lack"
GG Everything we know is bound up with absence and negation — with that which is not or appears not to be. Perhaps that's the most impressive thing about humans — that they have invented the concept of that which does not exist. The ability to portray ourselves in terms of those things that are antithetical to our own experience allows us not just a mathematical measure of the world in which we live but also a philosophical measure of who we are. Musical invention is bound up with negation; it is a dipping into the negation that lies outside the musical system from a position firmly ensconced in it. The foreground of musical composition has validity only insofar as it attempts to impose credibility on the vast background of human possibility that has yet to come into being. This is the role of the imagination, and without negation, imagination could not exist.
AS *Zwischenraum*
GG the space between, a gap, an unimaginable authority from which all meaning derives. It is a space that emerges with the music. There is no prefigured logic of harmony. Atonality produces shifting spaces, multi-locationalism, abandoning the single perspective of visual space. Like in your Moses opera, which exists between speaking and singing, notation and orchestration…

[Blue Self-Portrait *has been fading and is replaced by the 1911* Self-Portrait, *which shows Schoenberg from behind*]

AS Europe and America
GG Los Angeles
AS I like to swim…
GG …I named my boat the *Arnold S.*
AS it was either Los Angeles or New Zealand
GG but you chose L.A.
AS it had the musical advantage
GG and Brecht, Mann, Adorno, Stravinsky, Klemperer
AS as if I hadn't left [*said with a degree of scorn*]
GG and Shirley Temple across the street
AS I thought the tourists were looking at me
GG a stranger in a strange land
AS homeless
GG exiled
AS I was driven into paradise
GG did your family take to American ways?
AS my son became a tennis player
GG did he compete?
AS he was more famous at 12 than I was at 75!
GG you spent most of your time teaching
AS I told my students to write what was *possible* for their instruments, not what was *probable*
GG [pause] I never left Toronto
AS Toronto? where is this "Toronto"?
GG Toronto is in Canada
AS ah! *Canada!*
GG I grew up listening to records, and my greatest teacher was the tape recorder. The most important thing about growing up in Toronto was that it didn't have a classical music culture. What it had instead were great record stores. When it came time for me to perform, I tried to play what I had been hearing on records. Critics raved about my ability to separate the contrapuntal voices in the *Goldbergs* but I was simply trying to play what I had heard in my living room. I even worked the time it took to change records into my performance practice. In a sense my concert career was a blip; I didn't know it at the time, but my promised land was

the recording studio. It let me opt creatively out of the human situation
AS   transcendence?
GG   *ekstasis*

[*pause, in which GG plays in its entirety (circa 1 minute) the second of AS's* Six Little Piano Pieces *(op. 19)*]

AS   we are thrown into the world

[*begin to fade in the* Phantasy for Violin and Piano Accompaniment *(op. 47)*]

GG   yet we have art
AS   a cry of despair
GG   for one who experiences the fate of all mankind
AS   one must choose
GG   between old loyalties and new possibilities
AS   *Wer die Wahl hat, hat die Qual*
GG   he who has choice has torment
AS   the dilemma of Moses
GG   consonance and dissonance
AS   concept and belief
GG   beauty denying itself the illusion of beauty
AS   the music remains
GG   formal
AS   [*after a pause*] free

[*the* Phantasy *is still heard. At circa 2 minutes, the conversation having come to an end, Gould gets up and leaves the stage. At circa 1 minute, AS likewise. Lights have been gently dimming. We are left in a twilight for the last minute of music. Then lights slowly up as music fades out completely*]

Sources

AS   Bujić, Bojan. *Arnold Schoenberg*. London: Phaidon, 2011.
ASAP   Gould, Glenn. *Arnold Schoenberg: A Perspective*. Cincinnati: University of Cincinnati, 1964.
ASCJ   Ringer, Alexander L. *Arnold Schoenberg: The Composer as Jew*. Oxford: Clarendon, 1990.
ASJ   Shawn, Allen. *Arnold Schoenberg's Journey*. New York: FSG, 2002.
"ASSA"   HaCohen, Ruth. "Arnold Schoenberg: Sonic Allegories." In *Makers of Jewish Modernity*, edited by Jacques Picard et al., 173–86. Princeton: Princeton University Press, 2016.
CD   Brand, Juliane, and Christopher Hailey, eds. *Creative Dissonance: Arnold Schoenberg and the Transformations of Twentieth-Century Culture*. Berkeley: University of California Press, 1997.
DFD   Schoenberg, E. Randol, ed. *The Doctor Faustus Dossier*. Translated by Adrian Feuchtwanger and Barbara Zeigl Schoenberg. Oakland: University of California Press, 2018.
FDSV   Schorske, Carl. *Fin-de-Siècle Vienna: Politics and Culture*. New York: Knopf, 1980.
GGR   Page, Tim, ed. *The Glenn Gould Reader*. Toronto: Lester & Orpen Dennys, 1984.

L Schoenberg, Arnold. *Arnold Schoenberg Letters.* Edited by Erwin Stein. Translated by Eithne Wilkins and Ernst Kaiser. New York: St. Martin's Press, 1965.

M&A Wörner, Karl H. *Schoenberg's "Moses and Aaron."* Translated by Paul Hamburger, with the complete libretto in German and English. London: Faber and Faber, 1963.

MC Holl, Ute. *The Moses Complex: Freud, Schoenberg, Straub/Huillet.* Translated by Michael Turnbull. Zurich and Berlin: Diaphanes, 2017.

MS Cavell, Richard. *McLuhan in Space: A Cultural Geography.* Toronto: University of Toronto Press, 2002.

S Rosen, Charles. *Schoenberg.* London: Fontana, 1976.

SAHM Marcus, Kenneth H. *Schoenberg and Hollywood Modernism.* Cambridge: Cambridge University Press, 2015.

S&I Schoenberg, Arnold. *Style and Idea: Selected Writings.* Edited by Leonard Stein. Berkeley: University of California Press, 1984.

S&R Brown, Julie. *Schoenberg and Redemption.* Cambridge: Cambridge University Press, 2014.

SLWW Stuckenschmidt, H.H. *Schoenberg: His Life, World, and Work.* Translated by Humphrey Searle. London: Calder, 1977.

SRDL Auner, Joseph, ed. *A Schoenberg Reader: Documents of a Life.* New Haven: Yale University Press, 2003.

THR Sealey, Mark. "*Theory of Harmony* Review." *Classical Net*, 2010. http://www.classical.net/music/books/reviews/0520266080a.php.

WBW Barman, Jean. *The West Beyond the West: A History of British Columbia.* Toronto: University of Toronto Press, 1991.

WP Bahr, Erhard. *Weimar on the Pacific: German Exile Culture in Los Angeles and the Crisis of Modernism.* Berkeley: University of California Press, 2007.

WS Bazzana, Kevin. *Wondrous Strange: The Life and Art of Glenn Gould.* Toronto: McClelland and Stewart, 2003.

Act One

page 24
to stop singing! SLWW 97
Thalberg WP 270; SLWW 412–13
wondering S&I 484
not modern S 59
laboratory AS 112
expectations SLWW 315
space SLWW 525

page 25
a calf S&I 36; SRDL 281
shoveling snow S&R 2
movement FDSV 346
Lebensgefühl FDSV 347
nature…beautiful SRDL 93

page 26
alles rückgängig S&R 200
good ship post-Wagnerian GGR 125
perfecting my solitude S&I 30
aloof ASAP 13
dissolution SLWW 123
two notes AS 69

page 27
could not anticipate AS 68
it was lucky DFD 10
"contemporary" DFD 148
12 letters SLWW 409

page 28
first phrase GGR 197
The electronic age GGR 92
No work of art GGR 94

page 29
sensual and mystic AS 104
mystery GGR 113; ASAP 8
inconceivable M&A 113

Act Two

page 31
Gold WS 24
Jewish during the war WS 24
Franz Josef SLWW 452; AS 114

page 32
making an exception AS 115; SLWW 290
Germanic SLWW 370
west beyond WBW
flight WP 262
well-upholstered extension GGR 246

page 33
ear versus eye GGR 340
analytic clarity…tactile proximity GGR 333
cut as opposed to dissolve GGR 22
a longing SLWW 496
Bach…ever new GGR 113
what Bach taught us GGR 49

page 34
lives would be art GGR 353
a flow of information GGR 36
art is not technology GGR 86
rhythmic extenuations GGR 96
Brahms SLWW 355
Selfian SLWW 73
resemblance SLWW 337

page 35
Modernsky! AS 139
devil "ASSA" 178
emancipated L 253
synagogue noise "ASSA" 178
"chant mumbling" "ASSA" 178
speech is a form of music GGR 74
the *Odyssey* MC 59, quoting Kittler

page 36
Sprechgesang AS 88
"word that I lack" M&A 195
negation GGR 3
a gap MC 80
emerges with the music MC 302
multi-locationalism MS 160

page 37
Shirley Temple SAHM 141
homeless SLWW 393
driven into paradise AS 192
tennis; more famous SLWW 337
possible…probable SLWW 376–77
time to change records WS 97

page 38
opt creatively out GGR 326
thrown into the world "ASSA" 182, quoting Heidegger
despair ASCJ ix; SRDL 64
fate ASCJ ix
Wer die Wahl FDSV 351, quoting a German proverb
beauty "ASSA" 184–85, quoting Adorno

GLENN GOULD AND ARNOLD SCHOENBERG: *QUASI PARLANDO*

one

In his lifetime, the pianist Glenn Gould (1932–1982) was among the most prolific commentators on the work of composer Arnold Schoenberg (1874–1951) and among his most prominent performers.[1] As Yehudi Menuhin wrote in his autobiography, *Unfinished Journey,* "perhaps no one in the world knows as much about Schoenberg as Glenn does."[2] In addition to his commentaries on Schoenberg, Gould recorded all of the Schoenberg *Lieder,* all of the piano music, a number of the chamber works, and produced two documentaries on Schoenberg for the Canadian Broadcasting Corporation (CBC). Gould was a brilliant analyst of tone rows,[3] and Gould's own string quartet — his one musical composition — sounds like a work by the Schoenberg

---

[1] Geoffrey Payzant states that Gould in his lifetime was the most prolific commentator on Schoenberg; see *Glenn Gould: Music and Mind* (Toronto: Van Nostrand Reinhold, 1978), 142. James K. Wright argues that "Gould was the most passionate [...] of [...] Canadian Schoenbergians" and notes that "Gould performed and recorded Schoenberg's music more than any other musician of his stature." See "Glenn Gould, Arnold Schoenberg, and Soviet Reception of the Second Viennese School," *Schoenberg's Chamber Music, Schoenberg's World,* eds. James K. Wright and Alan M. Gillmor (Hillsdale: Pendragon Press, 2009), 237–38.

[2] Yehudi Menuhin, *Unfinished Journey* (New York: Knopf, 1997), 333.

[3] Kevin Bazzana, *Glenn Gould: The Performer in the Work* (Oxford: Clarendon Press, 1997), 88.

who wrote *Verklärte Nacht*. This manifest interest in "the man who changed music" (the title of one of Gould's radio documentaries on Schoenberg) was developed while Gould was making his name as one of the foremost keyboard interpreters of Bach, starting with his legendary 1955 recording of the *Goldberg Variations,* performances which came to overshadow Gould's championing of Schoenberg. For Gould, however, this interest in Bach did not contradict his interest in Schoenberg, for both Bach and Schoenberg had worked within strictly delimited ideas of musical composition. If Bach was an important figure for Gould, it was "Bach seen through the eyes of Schoenberg," as Kevin Bazzana has put it.[4]

Despite the prolixity of Gould's commentaries on Schoenberg, Gould is little cited in current research on the composer. In part, this is because Gould's understanding of Schoenberg was based on sources — primarily René Leibowitz — that are now considered dated. As well, Gould's highly eccentric style of writing has tended to make his essays of less interest to Schoenberg scholars than to those interested in Gould. However, Gould's writings on Schoenberg are important for a number of reasons: they argue the significance of the mediatic context — specifically sound recording — in which Schoenberg's music was written; they alert us to the fact that Schoenberg's legacy is not exclusively in the twelve-tone system of composition that he pioneered, but in the creation of a musical (and, more broadly, artistic) environment that extends into the domains of theater and performance, film music and rap;[5] and they

---

4   Ibid., 21. Bazzana perhaps means to stress the clarity, articulation, and restraint that Gould brought to his playing of Bach, which becomes highly evident when one compares either of his recordings of the *Goldbergs* with a harpsichord performance, such as that of Yoshiko Ieki (Regulus 2018).

5   In his review of the London production of Lin-Manuel Miranda's *Hamilton,* Colin Grant writes that "*Hamilton*'s hip-hop confidently sweeps aside the question that often lurks in the mind of novice musical-goers: why has the cast broken into song? For rap is essentially a spoken word art form, closer to speech than singing." See Colin Grant, "The Theatre Where It Happens," *The Times Literary Supplement,* January 10, 2018, https://www.the-tls.co.uk/articles/public/the-theatre-where-it-happens/. Kyle Adams

demonstrate that much of what we now listen to in classical and post-classical music we listen to with Schoenbergian ears. As a result, Gould's writings on Schoenberg open up a number of the Viennese composer's works to further consideration, especially *Moses und Aron,* which emerges from a Gouldian perspective as a meditation on music and mediation. It is in this context that *Speechsong* seeks to intervene, taking the juxtaposition of speaking and singing that defines *Sprechstimme*—a form of vocal performance between speaking and singing— as indicative of the larger concerns that Schoenberg and Gould held to be important.

Schoenberg and Gould had complicated relationships to performance.[6] Gould famously recused himself from the stage in 1964, devoting himself thereafter to sound recordings in which his "performance" was electronically constructed through the process of tape splicing rather than simply registered analogically—Gould made 282 outtakes for the 38 minute recording of the 1955 *Goldberg Variations.*[7] The second half of the Menuhin quote above continues "or [knows] more than he [Gould]

---

notes that "although rap lyrics are spoken, rappers still manipulate pitch for expressive purposes, sometimes within single words. [...] In the pitch domain, the analyst must [...] choose between a faithful, Sprechstimme-style representation of the lyrics, or choose to ignore variations in pitch at the expense of an accurate representation of the flow." See "The Musical Analysis of Hip-Hop," in *The Cambridge Companion to Hip-Hop,* ed. Justin A. Williams (Cambridge: Cambridge University Press, 2015), 121. What is significant in the use of both rap and *Sprechstimme* is the relationship to hybridity as well as an implied critique of established forms of singing, be they *bel canto* or rock. Schoenberg's student Lou Harrison's use of *Sprechgesang* in the "Three Coyote Stories" of his *Last Symphony* provides a crucial link to contemporary manifestations such as those in *Hamilton.*

6 Wright states that "Gould was [...] strongly opposed to all forms of musical showmanship" and that he "dismissed some of the most celebrated pianists of the twentieth century [...] as 'demonic virtuosi'" ("Glenn Gould," 238 and note 6).

7 All 282 tracks of Gould's outtakes for the *Goldbergs* have now been issued by Sony Classical in five discs, accompanied by an 80-page booklet. See Anthony Tommasini, "Glenn Gould's Treasures for the Taking," *The New York Times: Arts and Leisure,* February, 4 2018, 8.

does about the recording and broadcasting of music,"⁸ and Gould makes the connection between recording and Schoenberg explicit when he writes that "Schoenberg's music, especially his later works, which so decisively influenced the compositional climate of the present day, are suited to the medium of recording."⁹ As John P.L. Roberts notes, "Gould was the first performing musician to develop an aesthetic totally in terms of the electronic media, and in terms of recordings in particular."¹⁰ Furthermore, Gould's "performances" were a form of composition (sometimes literally), in which he became a "co-creator" with the composer. Schoenberg was not primarily a performer, and his works are oriented more to a theoretical rather than a performative logic. Like Gould, he was somewhat of a musical autodidact,¹¹ having had only a brief tutelage from the musician Alexander von Zemlinsky. Gould, for his part, tended to repudiate what his one teacher, Alberto Guerrero, had taught him. As he said in an interview, "I came to dislike what [his] style of piano playing represented."¹² The most famous moment in Gould's

---

8   Menuhin, *Unfinished Journey*, 333.
9   Quoted by Payzant, *Glenn Gould*, 45–46, from a 1967 CBC broadcast.
10 John P.L. Roberts, "Preface," in *Glenn Gould: Selected Letters,* eds. John P.L. Roberts and Ghyslaine Guertin (Toronto: Oxford University Press, 1992), xi.
11 Richard Taruskin notes the paradox of the fact that "one of the outstanding academic music theorists and composition teachers of the twentieth century was himself self-taught." See chapter 6 of the section on modernism, part 1 ("Rejecting Success") in *The Oxford History of Modern Music* at http://www.oxfordwesternmusic.com. Charles Rosen, however, urges caution with this notion. As he states, "Schoenberg, who was playing the violin and composing at the age of eight, is often described as an autodidact because he did not attend a music school — as if composers ever learned much of their trade in such schools anyway, and as if the help he received when he was seventeen from his friend Alexander von Zemlinsky, who *was* attending music school, did not give him all the teaching he needed." See *Schoenberg* (London: Fontana/Collins, 1976), 75.
12 Glenn Gould, "Interview with Alan Rich," in *The Art of Glenn Gould,* ed. John P.L. Roberts (Toronto: Malcolm Lester Books, 1999), 138. Nevertheless, Gould's performance practices owed a considerable amount to Guerrero. John Beckwith remarks that "Gould learned most of his technical habits from Guerrero, though he eventually willfully rejected

performance career was, paradoxically, his abandonment of the concert hall. This happened on April 10, 1964, in the Wilshire Ebell Theater in Los Angeles. *Speechsong* originated there: when I opened the lobby door on a visit in 1989, the first thing I saw was a large photographic portrait of Schoenberg hanging on the wall.[13] Clearly, Gould had been saying goodbye to Schoenberg, the Schoenberg who had so profoundly changed the relationship of the performer not simply to the audience but to the very idea of performativity and the listening environment.

Gould — one of the first persons in Toronto to own a tape recorder[14] — grew up in a city that was the media capital of Canada, location of the recording studios of the CBC in which Gould would spend much of his life after 1964. And Toronto was an eight-hour drive from New York, the media capital of the world. It was there that Gould had made the 1955 recording of the *Goldberg Variations* that catapulted him onto the world stage — that other, global stage,[15] theorized most notably by his Toronto confrère, Marshall McLuhan. Gould was deeply influenced by McLuhan. While notoriously reclusive, Gould would visit McLuhan at his Wells Hill Avenue home, a twenty-minute

---

many of Guerrero's aesthetic and interpretive ideas." See *In Search of Alberto Guerrero* (Waterloo: Wilfrid Laurier University Press, 2006), 104–5. In his native Chile, Guerrero was an early proponent of Schoenberg.

13 The ceremony awarding Schoenberg an honorary Viennese citizenship took place at the Ebell in 1949. His *Prelude* to Nathaniel Shilkret's *Genesis Suite* was performed at the Ebell on November 18, 1945, and his *Three Folksongs for Mixed Chorus* on June 27, 1949. See Kenneth H. Marcus, *Schoenberg and Hollywood Modernism* (Cambridge: Cambridge University Press, 2016), 239; 284–85. Sabine Feisst in *Schoenberg's New World: The American Years* (Oxford: Oxford University Press, 2011) details the many performances of Schoenberg's works in Los Angeles during his residence there.

14 Roberts, *The Art of Glenn Gould*, 233.

15 In 1972, McLuhan, with Barrington Nevitt, wrote of "the institution of a new kind of global theater, in which all [persons] become actors and there are few spectators." See *Take Today: The Executive as Dropout* (Toronto: Longman, 1972), 145.

walk from Gould's St. Clair Avenue penthouse.[16] We know they talked about music and technology because they collaborated on a dialogue about this topic, and a number of Gould's ideas about music and technology bear strong evidence of McLuhan's media theories.

Gould's "Dialogue on the Prospects of Recording" was aired first on the CBC radio network in January of 1965. Subsequently, McLuhan published it in the "Explorations" series that he edited for the University of Toronto's *Varsity Graduate* (April 1965). Gould then republished it as an article in *High Fidelity* magazine (April 1966). In the article, Gould predicts that the "public concert as we know it today would no longer exist a century hence."[17] Here we see Gould making a prediction that is clearly aligned with McLuhan's notion that book culture was coming to an end as we enter into the acoustic environment produced by electronic media, and at the same time channeling McLuhan's polemical tone. Gould goes on to state that "a recent brief prepared by the University of Toronto's department of musicology proposing a computer-controlled phonographic information system succinctly noted [that] 'Whether we recognize it or not, the long-playing record has come to embody the very reality of music.'"[18] Gould states that "[t]oday's listeners have come to associate musical performance with sounds possessed of characteristics which two generations ago were neither available to the profession nor wanted by the public — characteristics such as analytic clarity, immediacy, and indeed almost tactile proximity."[19] The word "tactile" is a clear McLuhan reference; the media theorist associated tactility with electronic media, which were multi-sensually oriented, unlike print, which privi-

---

16 Choreographer Vanessa Goodman has produced a dance piece based on the Gould/McLuhan nexus called *Wells Hill*. See https://www.sfu.ca/sfuwoodwards/events/events1/summer-2017/ActionAtADistance-WellsHill.html.
17 Glenn Gould, "The Prospects of Recording," in *The Glenn Gould Reader*, ed. Tim Page (Toronto: Lester & Orpen Dennys, 1984), 331.
18 Ibid., 332.
19 Ibid., 333.

leged the eyes over the other sensory organs. Electronic media, in contrast, put the senses in touch with each other through their deeply involving power. While this sounded counterintuitive to McLuhan's 1960s audiences, we now live in an era when touching screens is a fact of life. "Tactility," of course, would have had special significance for a pianist, suggesting a powerful relationship between the "secondary orality"[20] of electronic media and recorded piano performance. Of particular note in the article is Gould's comment that arguments against recording (he was often critiqued for abandoning the stage, including by Menuhin), as opposed to concertizing, derived from "eye versus ear orientation."[21] This is another McLuhanesque notion — that with the decline of print culture and the ascendancy of electronic media we were getting an "ear" for an "eye."[22] While print is a mechanical medium, electronic media are organic and embodied. As Frances Dyson has noted, "one always hears with one's body, and that body is permeated by sound."[23] The prominence that Schoenberg gave to *Sprechstimme,* from *Pierrot Lunaire* to *Moses und Aron,* was very much a harbinger of this embodied, acoustic, mediated space.

McLuhan argued that Schoenberg, in embracing acoustic space, had "abandoned the visual structures of tonality in composition for the 'multi-locationalism' of atonality."[24] As he put it:

> Atonality in music represents the abandonment of the 'central key,' that is, of a single perspective or organizing frame

---

20 Walter J. Ong (McLuhan's student) writes about secondary orality in *Orality and Literacy: The Technologizing of the Word* (New York: Methuen, 1982), 133.
21 Gould, "The Prospects of Recording," 340.
22 Marshall McLuhan and Quentin Fiore, *The Medium Is the Massage: An Inventory of Effects* (New York: Random House, 1967), 121.
23 Frances Dyson, "The Ear That Would Hear Sounds In Themselves: John Cage 1945–1965," in *Wireless Imagination: Sound, Radio and the Avant-Garde,* eds. Douglas Kahn and Gregory Whitehead (Cambridge: MIT Press, 1992), 387.
24 Marshall McLuhan and Eric McLuhan, *Laws of Media: The New Science* (Toronto: University of Toronto Press, 1988), 52.

to which all elements of a composition are related. [...] [T]onality served as a figure to which to relate other figures in an abstract way: in the mosaic of acoustic space, each element creates its own space. [...] Using atonality [...] (as in acoustic space), 'wherever you are at the moment' is the key you're in, the tonal center, and the governing consideration is the nature of and effect on the overall pattern. Such space is not uniform but rather a multidimensional dynamic of figure and ground.[25]

Whereas in the concert hall, the pianist occupied the space of figure and the audience of ground, in recordings that space is in constant flux — dialogical. Hence McLuhan's comment that

Schönberg [sic] and Stravinsky and Carl Orff, far from being advanced seekers of esoteric effects, seem now to have brought music very close to the condition of ordinary human speech. It is this colloquial rhythm that once seemed so unmelodious about their work. Anyone who listens to the medieval works of Perotinus or Dufay will find them very close to Stravinsky and Bartok. The great explosion of the Renaissance that split musical instruments off from song and speech and gave them specialist functions is now being played backward in our age of electronic implosion.[26]

This passage gains considerable weight in the context of Schoenberg's *Second String Quartet* (op. 10), where the soprano's voice in the third and fourth movements is so unusual and compelling.

---

[25] Ibid. Compare Carl Schorske, who writes that for Schoenberg "the firm traditional coordinates of ordered time and space were losing their reliability, perhaps even their truth." See *Fin-de-Siècle Vienna: Politics and Culture* (New York: Knopf, 1980), 345.

[26] Marshall McLuhan, *Understanding Media: The Extensions of Man* (New York: McGraw-Hill, 1964), 328.

two

Canadian political abjection — the ongoing "identity" crisis of one of the oldest continuous democratic federations in the world[1] — has long extended to the cultural domain, where it manifests itself as the pathologization of genius. Hence, Gould's brilliant pianism must be a form of autism,[2] and McLuhan's staggering intellect must derive from an additional carotid artery.[3] Whatever the claims that can be made for these theses, they belie more salient facts: that Gould reconfigured musical performance for an audience weaned on recordings, and that McLuhan's dictum "the medium is the message" issued a profound challenge to Western philosophy, both epistemologically and ontologically. Not only did he disrupt the notion that knowledge was independent of its medium, but he also questioned notions of the sovereign self with the suggestion that our being

---

1   This is the claim of John Ralston Saul, "Canada 160 Years Later," *Globe and Mail,* March 11, 2008, https://www.theglobeandmail.com/opinion/canada-160-years-later/article718521/.
2   See S. Timothy Maloney, "Glenn Gould, Autistic Savant," in *Sounding Off: Theorizing Disability in Music,* eds. Neil Lerner and Joseph Straus (New York: Routledge, 2006), 121–36, and, more broadly, Peter Ostwald, *Glenn Gould: The Ecstasy and Tragedy of Genius* (New York: Norton, 1998).
3   See Douglas Coupland, *Marshall McLuhan* (Toronto: Penguin, 2009), 35, 64–67, and 214.

had been inverted by electric technologies, such that our self-understanding was now outside ourselves — we had become what we beheld, as McLuhan often said. Gould understood these distinctions intuitively, and it should come as no surprise that he summed up his "incarceration" in the recording studio as "opting creatively out of the human situation."[4]

Here we approach the paradox of a performer who is seen as the embodiment of a humanist tradition that has one of its highpoints in the music of J.S. Bach. What we are hearing on those recordings, however, is not Gould playing; rather, we are hearing a technological (re)production of Gould playing. Giorgio Agamben seizes upon this notion as crucial to Gould's musical philosophy: "his mastery conserves and exercises in the act not his potential to play [...] but rather his potential to not-play."[5] To put this mediatically (extrapolating from Agamben's argument about Gould's habit of not rehearsing), what we are hearing in a Gould recording is not Gould playing but a product of technology, because the recording is a myriad of splices. It is out of this encounter with technology that Gould produced his utterly compelling art. To McLuhan's dark vision of the technological mediascape, Gould replied by bringing beauty out of the maelstrom. Unlike the humanistic Gould that much of the criticism that has grown up around him wishes to promulgate, Gould was much more the "solitary outlaw" that B.W. Powe has described,[6] and hence Gould's comment in his self-interview that he would "like to try [his] hand at being a prisoner."[7]

If Gould's maelstrom was the social, political and cultural implosion associated with the 1960s, Schoenberg's vortex was defined by those modernist upheavals that we associate with Se-

---

4 Glenn Gould, "Glenn Gould Interviews Glenn Gould about Glenn Gould," in *The Glenn Gould Reader*, ed. Tim Page (Toronto: Lester & Orpen Dennys, 1984), 326.
5 Giorgio Agamben, *The Coming Community*, trans. Michael Hardt (Minneapolis: University of Minnesota Press, 1993), 36.
6 Bruce W. Powe, "A Search for Glenn Gould," in *The Solitary Outlaw* (Toronto: Lester & Orpen Dennys, 1987), 135–65.
7 Gould, "Glenn Gould Interviews Glenn Gould about Glenn Gould," 326.

cessionism, Dada, Die Brücke, and so on, as well as by the rise of Nazism. As Carl Schorske suggests in *Fin-de-Siècle Vienna,* the artists involved with these movements were blindsided to the rise of Nazism precisely by the notion that their art was all-encompassing. "Vienna in the fin-de-siècle [...] proved one of the most fertile breeding grounds of our century's a-historical culture"[8] he writes. Indeed, Schorske goes on to note, "the very multiplicity of analytic categories by which modern movements defined themselves had become, to use Arnold Schoenberg's term, 'a death-dance of principles.'"[9] Yet it was through their "eruptive outburst against the aestheticism of the *fin-de-siècle,*" writes Shorske, that artists such as Schoenberg and Kokoschka "devised new languages in painting and music to proclaim the universality of suffering in transcendent negation of the professed values of their society. With the definition of modern man as one 'condemned to re-create his own universe,' twentieth-century Viennese culture had found its voice."[10] For Schorske, Schoenberg's abandonment of tonality was itself a political act, and manifested itself profoundly in *Sprechstimme,* his "agitated free verse — part speech, part song, part simply cry."[11]

---

8   Carl Schorske, *Fin-de-Siècle: Politics and Culture* (New York: Knopf, 1980), xviii.
9   Ibid., xix.
10 Ibid., xxix, internal quote from Oskar Kokoschka.
11 Ibid., 354.

three

The Vienna *fin-de-siècle* coincided with a shift from "art" to media, that is, a shift from a notion of art as subjective expression whereby the medium of that expression is subordinate to the idea expressed in the artwork, to the idea that the medium is itself the message (to allude to McLuhan's dictum), such that the artwork comes into being as an exploration of the medium itself. What occasioned this shift was the materialization of mediation in technologies such as photography, film, and the gramophone, which were becoming inescapable influences not only on art and communication but also for the understanding of being itself — if the human voice could be heard singing when a needle runs along a shellac disc, then the idea of the human was placed in question. As Friedrich Kittler writes, "[m]edia [...] correlate in the real itself to the materiality they deal with. Photo plates inscribe chemical traces of light, phonograph records inscribe the mechanical traces of sound."[1] One of the major distinctions of recording, as opposed to written notations, is that whereas the latter "effectively act as a filter that prevents noise, wrong notes, extraneous sounds [...] from entering into circulation," the for-

---

[1] Friedrich Kittler, "World-Breath: On Wagner's Media Technology," in *Opera through Other Eyes*, ed. David J. Levin (Stanford: Stanford University Press, 1994), 215–16.

mer "has no such filter mechanism. It records the sound wave, warts and all. Neither quality nor intended meaning makes a difference to the recording. Sound is recorded qua sound."[2] Music entered into an expanded field with recording, and with that its norms became contested — it began to experience itself in terms of the medium of sound.[3]

The great harbinger in philosophy of the shift to mediation was Nietzsche's *Birth of Tragedy out of the Spirit of Music* (1872), which focused precisely on the role of "the medium of music" ("das Medium der Musik")[4] in this shift, as exemplified by Wagner's operas. Wagner was crucial to this move toward an understanding of music as a material medium in its own right through his embrace of acoustic space. As Kittler puts it, "Wagner's new medium, sound, breaks with 600 years of literality or literature,"[5] which is to say that it breaks with the musicological understanding of music that coincided with the rise of literacy. Kittler has stated that Nietzsche inaugurated media philosophy with his comment that "our writing tools are also working on our thoughts,"[6] a comment Nietzsche made when he realized that his use of a typewriter wasn't simply transcribing his words

---

2   Alexander Rehding, "Introduction: Discrete/Continuous: Music and Media Theory after Kittler: A Colloquy," *Journal of the American Musicological Society* 70, no. 1 (2017): 223.
3   Lucy Shanno argues that "Schoenberg capitalized on the repeatability of recording to produce compositional and hermeneutic difficulty." See "Composing with Recording in Mind: An Analytic Approach," abstract of PhD diss., University of Pennsylvania, 2007, https://repository.upenn.edu/dissertations/AAI3271813.
4   Friedrich Nietzsche, *The Birth of Tragedy out of the Spirit of Music*, trans. Douglas Smith (Oxford: Oxford University Press, 2000), 41. For the German text see http://www.nietzschesource.org/#eKGWB/GT. The first version of *The Birth* presents itself as a pro-Wagner screed but was subsequently re-issued as an anti-Wagner polemic. A quarter of a century before Nietzsche's *Birth of Tragedy*, "mediation" acquired the additional meaning, in English, of "that part of plain song that lies between two reciting notes" (*OED*; this meaning is dated 1845).
5   Kittler, "World-Breath," 226.
6   Quoted by Friedrich Kittler in *Gramophone Film Typewriter*, trans. Geoffrey Winthrop-Young and Michael Wutz (Stanford: Stanford University Press, 1999), 200.

but actively mediating them, giving them a mode of expression they otherwise would not have. (His use of the typewriter was occasioned by his increasing loss of sight; he couldn't see the paper but he could memorize the location of the keys to type.)[7] In writing *The Birth of Tragedy*, Nietzsche had sought to reverse the shift from *akouein* to *theōria* (from acoustic modes to visual modes) that had been precipitated in philosophy by the rise of literacy.[8] In musing about the implications of the return of opera to the European stage, Nietzsche was highlighting the transition, after 500 years of visual culture,[9] to a new embrace of the acoustic — a shift from the Apollonian to the Dionysian, from the visual domain to "the shattering force of sound."[10] It was this association of Dionysian ecstasy — *ekstasis*, or being outside oneself — with a return to acoustic culture that likewise informed McLuhan's concept of an electronically produced acoustic space and of media as prosthetic extensions of the body, and — with electronic media — of consciousness itself.

As Kittler reminds us, gramophone, film, and typewriter were asserting their effects at the turn from the 19th to the 20th century. All three media pronounced the end of the domain of written representation and the beginning of a new *nomos*,[11] in which sound (in the case of the gramophone) and acoustic (non-linear) space generally would supersede written and, more broadly, visual (perspectival) space. This move away from linearity in the context of musical production indicated a move away from representation, which is to say a move away from tonality, from the narrative notion that a musical "story" must resolve itself with a conclusion that ties up loose ends, such that

---

7 Early typewriters did not permit one to see what was being typed, a history traced by Kittler in *Gramophone Film Typewriter*.
8 I draw here on Richard Cavell, "The Tragedy of Media: Nietzsche, McLuhan, Kittler," in *Remediating McLuhan* (Amsterdam: Amsterdam University Press, 2016), 127–51.
9 The Greek word *theōria* (θεωρία) means "speculation."
10 Nietzsche, *The Birth of Tragedy out of the Spirit of Music*, 26.
11 *Nomos* refers both to a set of laws and to the melodies used by the singers of epics. The connection is that laws were promulgated by being sung in the *agora*.

the story predominates over the medium of representation. The representational aspect of music, in its most extreme version, takes the form of program music, in which music represents aspects of the "real" world, as in the *William Tell Overture* (1829), where we first "hear" the drops of rain and then get to experience the full storm, thanks to the concerted efforts of the trombonists. Wagner took this notion to its logical conclusion, such that *Tristan und Isolde* (whose score he referred to as a "plot" [*eine Handlung*]")[12] moves irrevocably to tonal and structural resolution in the last moment of the *Liebestod*.

What Schoenberg realized was that this resolution was belied by the work as a whole, in that the work was based on a continual *refusal* of tonal harmony, and on harmonic suspension, until the last note. In terms of Jacques Lacan's theory of signification, the superfoetation of signifiers in the *Liebestod* represents a "lack" (*manque*), a desire for being which continually escapes it.[13] Schoenberg approached this paradox through a form of designification;[14] if "the voice is the excess of the signifier,"[15] as Mladen Dolar argues, then Schoenberg would remove that excess via *Sprechstimme,* which sings but not quite, thereby returning the musical signifiers to the mathematical relations that were at the origin of musical expression. As Kittler puts it, "[b]y the time Schoenberg, in 1910, produced the last analysis of harmony in the history of music, chords had turned into pure acoustics,"[16] a set of mathematical relations. This was the function of the twelve-tone system. It allowed Schoenberg

---

12 Richard Wagner, *Tristan und Isolde: Handlung in drei Aufzügen* (Frankfurt: Insel, 2000).
13 Jacques Lacan, *Écrits: A Selection,* trans. Alan Sheridan (London: Tavistock, 1977), 281.
14 Designification can also be understood as a function of memory loss; the ultimate loss of memory in the Moses story is that of the origin of Moses himself, as both Freud and Jan Assmann remind us. For "designification" see Edward Jayne, "Metaphoric Hypersignification, Metonymic Designification," *Centennial Review* 38, no. 1 (1994): 9–32.
15 Mladen Dolar, *A Voice and Nothing More* (Cambridge: MIT Press, 2006), 81.
16 Kittler, *Gramophone Film Typewriter,* 24.

to ask what a work of music would sound like if it deliberately avoided tonic resolution. What would it sound like if it refused linear tonality and sequential structure and adopted a spatial structure instead, one in which musical meaning was produced relationally, rather than via tonic resolution? This became the basis for Schoenberg's tonic experiments that culminated in his compositions with twelve tones. Twelve tone composition created a new musical space;[17] rather than the linear one of tonal composition, whereby meaning would become evident in the tonal resolution, Schoenberg created a juxtapositional space,[18] whereby meaning was produced in the relationships between the notes.[19]

---

17 Richard Taruskin writes that "the most important (or at least the most fundamental) thing that the emancipation of dissonance vouchsafed was [...] the achievement of a fully integrated musical space." See the section on "Musical Space" in the 6th chapter ("Inner Occurrences") of *The Oxford History of Western Music,* http://www.oxfordwesternmusic.com.

18 Schoenberg made a number of row tables which he used in composition. As Kathryn Bailey comments, "the row tables were a [...] significant part of Schoenberg's creative process. [...] His tables were made in a wide variety of formats: cylinders, wheels, folded booklets, bound booklets, accordion-folded strips, two-color grids which are to be read in all directions, [...] sets of cards containing selected pairs of row forms, cut-outs and overlays, slide rules, window devices, circular devices, Scrabble-like letter squares, dice, and more." See "Webern's Row Tables," in *Webern Studies,* ed. Kathryn Bailey (Cambridge: Cambridge University Press, 1996), 224, and R. Wayne Shoaf and Susan L. Sloan's exhibition catalog, *Schoenberg's Dodecaphonic Devices* (Los Angeles: Arnold Schoenberg Institute, 1989).

19 This is not to deny that the form of a musical work exerts a linear pull. In his use of traditional forms such as the sonata, Schoenberg demonstrated the traditionalism that Gould had identified in his compositions. But Schoenberg can also be said to have been searching for new formal principles that were not teleologically linear. As Arved Ashby notes, Schoenberg "at the beginning of the third movement of the op. 26 *Wind Quintet,* in measures 1–7 of the horn line [...] had made a decisive breakthrough in the basic twelve-tone difficulty of reconciling the serial, linear imperative with the need for a consistent harmonic vocabulary." See "Schoenberg, Boulez, and Twelve-Tone Composition as 'Ideal Type,'" *Journal of the American Musicological Society* 54, no. 3 (2001): 596.

This relational notion of musical composition was a profound anticipation of digitality, which is performative by definition — coding, recoding, decoding — and it is digitality through which Gould's performance practices attain their ultimate significance, as in his second recording of the *Goldbergs*. As someone who encountered music largely via recordings, Gould sought to reproduce what he heard on records in his own playing. What he heard was a general "flattening" of the soundscape — a "relatively close-up, highly analytical sound."[20] Whereas the sound produced by the pianoforte is based on a three-dimensional, foreground/background spatial relation,[21] eminently suitable to the vast concert halls of the 19th century, recording technology is much more intimate and interactive, allowing the musical notes to exist juxtapositionally, each note in its own space. It is precisely this quality of articulation for which Gould's playing is famous. In effect, Gould saw the deep connections between Schoenberg's principles of composition and the performance practices that recording technologies facilitated.

Gould was highly critical of Pierre Boulez's *Schoenberg est mort*, published in 1952 (the year after Schoenberg's death), which argued that Schoenberg had failed to follow his compositional techniques to their logical conclusion, "backsliding" in his later works into tonality.[22] According to Gould, however, "Schoenberg had many more possibilities than have yet been

---

20 Glenn Gould, letter to Ronald Wilford, December 21, 1971, in *Glenn Gould: Selected Letters,* eds. John P.L. Roberts and Ghyslaine Guertin (Toronto: Oxford University Press, 1992), 170.
21 R. Murray Schafer writes that in "the music of the classical concert" the "real space of the concert hall is extended in[to] the virtual space of dynamics — by which effects may be brought into the foreground (forte) or allowed to drift back toward the acoustic horizon (piano)." See *The Tuning of the World* (New York: Knopf, 1977), 117.
22 Pierre Boulez, "Schoenberg Is Dead," in *Notes of an Apprenticeship,* trans. Herbert Weinstock (New York: Random House,1968), 268–75. The "exploration of the dodecaphonic realm may be bitterly held against Schoenberg, for it went off in the wrong direction so persistently that it would be hard to find an equally mistaken perspective in the entire history of music" (271).

exploited,"[23] a comment that derived from Gould's understanding that what Schoenberg had achieved was a new soundscape, a new way of listening, a new understanding of composition. In addition, Schoenberg had produced work that did not support an idea of musical performance that was part of the virtuoso tradition. This was not music composed for the concert hall and for social occasions that took on a greater importance than the music itself. The works he composed would be hard to listen to because they would actually *require* listening, listening to every note rather than listening for the *coup de grâce* of tonic resolution. In this context, what Schoenberg succeeded in creating was not just a body of musical compositions but a new musical environment, and it is this environment that we live in today. As Gould noted, Schoenberg's career is inseparable from the rise of recordings; his minutely articulated compositions would be lost in the concert hall[24] but are readily accessible via recordings, especially now, with the omnipresent use of headphones. Headphones remind us that music is embodied — it resonates within us — and it is this sense of embodiment that Gould is referring to in that famous passage where he states that in the best of all possible worlds, the audience would be the artist and their lives would be art.[25] This is not Romanticism — eschewed viscerally by both Schoenberg and Gould — but a deeply felt understanding of the involving effects of electronic media.

---

23 Glenn Gould, "Interview with Alan Rich," in *The Art of Glenn Gould,* ed. John P.L. Roberts (Toronto: Malcolm Lester Books, 1999), 143.

24 Gould wrote to Robert Craft on May 9, 1961 about the "wonderfully analytical clarity" of Craft's recording of Schoenberg's *Piano Concerto* (op. 42). See *Selected Letters,* 46.

25 "In the best of all possible worlds, art would be unnecessary. Its offer of restorative, placative therapy would go begging a patient. The professional specialization involved in its making would be presumption. The generalities of its applicability would be an affront. The audience would be the artist and their life would be art." See Glenn Gould, "The Prospects of Recording," in *The Glenn Gould Reader,* ed. Tim Page (Toronto: Lester & Orpen Dennys, 1984), 353.

four

While Gould's relationship to mediation was overt, Schoenberg's was more subtle. As Ute Holl suggests in *The Moses Complex: Freud, Schoenberg, Straub/Huillet*, Schoenberg's opera, *Moses und Aron,* is ultimately about "the transformation of the political under media conditions."[1] Focusing on Freud's and Schoenberg's readings of the Moses myth, and on the 1974 film of *Moses und Aron* made by Jean-Marie Straub and Danièle Huillet, Holl draws on Gregory Bateson's suggestion that to posit gods is to enter into cybernetics (a notion that Friedrich Kittler would take up), asserting that "Schoenberg [...] conceived his operas in the light of media aesthetics,"[2] addressing in *Moses und Aron* major questions of orality, literacy, freedom, and law.[3] As Holl puts it, "[f]rom the perspective of media studies, which is a science of differential relationships between materi-

---
1 Ute Holl, *The Moses Complex: Freud, Schoenberg, Straub/Huillet,* trans. Michael Turnbull (Zurich-Berlin: Diaphanes, 2017), 7.
2 Ibid., 11.
3 John Durham Peters states, in "The Ten Commandments as Media Theory," that "[a]ny theology of revelation is necessarily also a theory of media" (276) and that "[the third] commandment honors the key media divide of textuality and orality" (279). See *Communication and Social Life: Studies in Honor of Professor Esteban López-Escobar,* eds. Maxwell McCombs and Manuel Martín Algarra (Pamplona: Ediciones Universidad de Navarra, 2012), 275–84.

alities and immaterialities, noises and messages, channels and signals, apparatuses and perceptions, the relationship to God or gods turns out to be one between people and their systems of thought."[4] Media, in other words, are epistemic, in that they provide the framework for what we can know. In the twentieth century, media became overtly political; as Holl states (alluding to Kittler), "[p]ower in the twentieth century became a thing of media, codes, and channels,"[5] and we need only recall the WW2 career of Alan Turing (who was giving math lessons in Trinity Hall, Cambridge when McLuhan was writing his dissertation there)[6] to be reminded of this.

Facilitated by the new medium of recording, and influenced by the rise of musical nationalism, late nineteenth and early twentieth-century music became engaged in a process of retrieving the musical past, from Dvořák's *Slavonic Dances* (1878; 1886) to Bartók's *Eight Improvisations on Hungarian Peasant Tunes* (1920). This nationalist recidivism would take a number of political forms, including the claim that contemporary music was a degeneration of earlier musical achievements. To place Schoenberg in this context, it can be argued that he was retrieving the oral tradition itself, in its association with the vocalization of Semitic scripts. If the vocalization of Semitic scripts is their defining quality, then the struggle for the promised land which occupied Schoenberg in *Moses und Aron* can be understood in terms of a conflict between orality and literacy, between singing and speaking. In Schoenberg's time this conflict had been racialized: Semitic script, in which vowels are not notated, was deemed inferior to the Greek alphabet and its use of written vowels.[7] Through this tension, as Holl crucially remarks, "the

---

4   Holl, *The Moses Complex*, 14.
5   Ibid., 59.
6   See Richard Cavell, "McLuhan, Turing, and the Question of Determinism," in *Remediating McLuhan* (Amsterdam: Amsterdam University Press, 2016), 91–96.
7   This tension returns in Kittler's *Musik und Mathematik I* (2006), with its celebration of the Greek alphabet: "'Everyone can speak Greek who merely knows the letters [he writes], but not Egyptian and Semitic'" (quoted in

topos of the opera shifts from the problem of a prohibition of images [...] to the question of emerging media relationships."[8] This set of mediatic considerations provided the groundwork for Schoenberg's ultimate response to National Socialism: unable to command interest for his various political proposals, he produced a cultural one. As Holl remarks, "the German debate [...] was happy to exaggerate the opposition between vocalic and consonantal alphabets under various antecedents. In this constellation it becomes clear how precisely Arnold Schoenberg opens his opera *Moses und Aron,* in his use of a sung vocali[s]e and then consonant-saturated reply in the [...] form of *Sprechstimme.* [...] He doesn't counter the then virulent Aryanization of a Hellenistic discourse with an originally Semitic or Hebrew one, but through marking *lacking* structures, languages, and forms of perception, and in the modernism of a vocal art that seeks transition, not boundaries."[9]

The threat against modernist music was an integral part of the Nazi cultural regime. As Benjamin G. Martin notes in *The Nazi-Fascist New Order for European Culture,*

> Germany would soon challenge the Italian fascists in cultural areas where they had been striving for several years to secure a leading role, including classical music and cinema. [...] The first field in which Italy — and the rest of Europe — was confronted by a powerful German initiative was in the area of the pan-European organization of classical music. [...] The heart of the problem [as the Germans saw it] was the outsized role of the International Society for Contemporary Music (ISCM). Since its foundation in 1922, the ISCM had become a powerful force in European music. Its festivals promoted

---

Holl, *The Moses Complex,* 58). As Holl states, "[t]hrough this the Moses complex becomes virulent once again, and with it the long history of a European phantasm spanning vocalic and consonantal script, song and voice, knowledge and thought, and leaders and followers of signs" (ibid., 60).

8   Ibid., 52.
9   Ibid., 63, my emphasis.

avant-garde music — featuring premieres of pathbreaking works by composers like Alban Berg, Paul Hindemith, Arnold Schoenberg, Igor Stravinsky, and Anton Webern — and were known for their elite, cosmopolitan audiences.[10]

The Nazi response was to create the Reich Music Chamber (Reichsmusikkammer, RMK) and to appoint Richard Strauss as its head:

> Strauss's mandate as head of the Reich Music Chamber was to oversee the National Socialist reordering, or 'coordination' (*Gleichschaltung*), of German musical life. Founded as part of the Reich Chamber of Culture, alongside Chambers of Literature, Theater, the Visual Arts, Press, Radio, and Film, Strauss's Reich Music Chamber would fulfill the vision Hitler had outlined at the September 1933 Nazi Party Congress on Culture. [...] The Reich Music Chamber promised a self-regulating guild of musicians under the protection of the state, while embracing a nationalist, culturally conservative vision of German music. [...] Of course, not all German musicians were welcome to participate. The Nazis' April 1933 'Law for the Restoration of the Professional Civil Service,' which barred Jews from public-sector employment, was already being used to drive Jewish musicians from the country's many state-and city-supported orchestras and opera houses. The influential modernist Austrian and Jewish composer Arnold Schoenberg, forced from his post at Berlin's Academy of the Arts, was one of many politically or 'racially' persecuted composers and performers who fled into exile.[11]

The policies of the RMK stemmed from "the racist distinction between 'pure,' national (*arteigene*) and 'alien' (*artfremde*) art. One of the great crimes of musical modernism, by this logic,

---

10 Benjamin G. Martin, *The Nazi-Fascist New Order for European Culture* (Cambridge: Harvard University Press, 2017), 17–18.

11 Ibid., 19–20.

was its importation of racially foreign styles and rhythms into the spiritual body of German music, and its trends,"[12] and it is for this reason that the prime target of the Nazis was the International Society for Contemporary Music (ISCM). As Martin remarks, by the 1920s "the institution had attracted the ire of nationalists, who accused it in particular of promoting atonal and twelve-tone music, scorned by many conservatives and anti-Semites for its connection to Jewish composers like Arnold Schoenberg, who, as a radical atonal composer and a Jew, was the bête noir[e] of German-speaking antimodernist circles."[13]

Ruth HaCohen has argued that it is precisely the use of atonality that was Schoenberg's way of re-asserting his Jewishness[14] in the face of the attribution of "degeneracy" to Jewish art. This took its most virulent form in the music libel against the Jews, as articulated by Wagner's repellent diatribe *The Jew in Music* (*Das Judenthum in der Musik*), first published in 1850 under a pseudonym.[15] Wagner begins by asserting that a "'Hebraic art-taste'" is becoming dominant through Jewish control of commerce; the Jew "rules, and will rule, so long as Money remains the power before which all our doings and our dealings lose their force,"[16] including art. The purpose of Wagner's pamphlet is to condemn in general the "be-Jewing of modern art"[17] (*die*

---

12 Ibid., 20.
13 Ibid., 20–21.
14 Julie Brown has made what is in effect the opposite argument: that it was Jewish self-loathing that moved Schoenberg in the direction of atonality. She bases this argument largely on a "private essay" Schoenberg wrote in 1934 in response to the rise of Nazism titled "Every young Jew." The essay, however, is scathingly ironic, and does not support the conclusions that Brown draws from it. See *Schoenberg and Redemption* (Cambridge: Cambridge University Press, 2014), and the review of her book by Steven J. Cahn in *Music and Letters* 97, no. 4 (2016): 665–67.
15 Richard Wagner, *The Jew in Music,* trans. William Ashton Ellis (London: Kegan Paul, 1894), http://www.jrbooksonline.com/pdf_books/judaisminmusic.pdf.
16 Ibid., 7.
17 Ibid., 8.

Verjüdung der modernen Kunst),[18] and in particular its effect on music. As a "freak of Nature,"[19] the Jew is unrepresentable in visual art. More specifically to Wagner's argument, the Jew's "*speech [Sprache]*"[20] is such that the Jew is antithetical to music. "Our whole European art and civilisation," writes Wagner, "have remained to the Jew a foreign tongue."[21] In particular, "the first thing that strikes our ear as quite outlandish and unpleasant, in the Jew's production of the voice-sounds, is a creaking, squeaking, buzzing snuffle,"[22] an "intolerably jumbled blabber [*eines unerträglich verwirrten Geplappers*]"[23] This point, argues Wagner, has immense importance for "the impression made on us by the music-works of modern Jews": "If we hear a Jew speak, we are unconsciously offended by the entire want of purely-human expression in his discourse: the cold indifference of its peculiar 'blubber' never by any chance rises to the ardour of a higher, heartfelt passion."[24] Here Wagner arrives at his central point:

> Now, if the aforesaid qualities of his dialect make the Jew almost incapable of giving artistic enunciation to his feelings and beholdings through talk, for such an enunciation through song his aptitude must needs be infinitely smaller. *Song is just Talk aroused to highest passion*: Music is the speech of Passion. All that worked repellently upon us in his outward appearance and his speech, makes us take to our heels at last in his Song, providing we are not held prisoners by the very ridicule of this phenomenon. Very naturally, in Song — the vividest and most indisputable expression of

---

18 Richard Wagner, *Das Judenthum in der Musik* (Leipzig: Weber, 1869), 8, https://de.wikisource.org/wiki/Das_Judenthum_in_der_Musik_(1869).
19 Wagner, *The Jew in Music*, 9.
20 Ibid., 11; Wagner, *Das Judenthum in der Musik*, 11.
21 Wagner, *The Jew in Music*, 14.
22 Ibid.
23 Ibid., 15; Wagner, *Das Judenthum in der Musik*, 15.
24 Wagner, *The Jew in Music*, 15.

the personal emotional-being — the peculiarity of the Jewish nature attains for us its climax of distastefulness.[25]

Having made this point, Wagner confronts an apparent paradox: some Jews have become musicians. The explanation of this paradox, states Wagner, is money. As culture has increasingly become driven by money, the Jew uses money to assert a cultural presence, but as Thinkers, not as Poets: "the Thinker is the backward-looking poet; but the true Poet is the foretelling Prophet."[26] These are terms that resonate with *Moses und Aron,* as does Wagner's emphasis on speaking and singing. Since all art must come from the Folk, Jews have no recourse in their music making but to turn to "the ceremonial music of their Jehovah-rites: the Synagogue is the solitary fountain whence the Jew can draw art-motives at once popular and intelligible to himself."[27] Yet all the Synagogue can offer is a "sense-and-sound-confounding gurgle, yodel and cackle [*Gegurgels, Gejodels und Geplappers*]"[28] such that the "rhythms and melismi of the Synagogue-song usurp his musical fancy [*Jene Melismen und Rhythmen des Synagogengesanges nehmen seine musikalische Phantasie*]."[29] Wagner concludes from this that "What issues from the Jews' attempts at making Art, must necessarily therefore bear the attributes of coldness and indifference, even to triviality and absurdity; and in the history of Modern Music we can but class the Judaic period as that of final unproductivity, of stability gone to ruin."[30]

The prime example of this lack of musical talent is Felix Mendelssohn Bartholdy, according to Wagner, whose works are all surface, without any depth, as in those works where Mendelssohn mimics Bach — but only his formal qualities, not his feeling. (Throughout this section, the word "speech" [*Sprache*]

---

25 Ibid., 15–16, my emphasis.
26 Ibid., 17.
27 Ibid., 19.
28 Ibid., 19; Wagner, *Das Judenthum in der Musik,* 22.
29 Wagner, *The Jew in Music,* 20; Wagner, *Das Judenthum in der Musik,* 22.
30 Wagner, *The Jew in Music,* 23.

is used to describe the musical idiom, such as "Bach's musical speech" [*Bachs musikalische Sprache*]).³¹ Wagner likewise castigates Giacomo Meyerbeer (whom he does not deign to name), concluding that the only way the Jew can redeem himself (other than through self-annihilation) is to follow the example of Ahasuerus, the eternally wandering Jew. As Julie Brown has noted, Schoenberg commented directly on this passage, stating that this notion of the wandering Jew as representative of all Jews is in fact a Christian construct: "Ahasver [Ahasuerus], the justifiably persecuted Jew, exists only for Christians, not for Jews."³² What Schoenberg had in mind in response to Wagner's diatribe, in fact, was precisely the opposite of what Wagner proposed: rather than seeking to deny his musical heritage, Schoenberg would embrace the very "noise" that Wagner had condemned.

This is the thesis of Ruth HaCohen:

> I propose to view his [Schoenberg's] creative journey as a highly profound, though only partially conscious, modernist endeavor to grapple with the complexity of the music libel against the Jews, through various vocal fictions — oratorical, lyrical, and dramatic. This goes beyond his famous "emancipation of the dissonance" enterprise, as it is usually understood, that is, in terms of expanding the tonal universe and the evening-out of all tonal combinations. The term (coined by Schoenberg himself) can be seen, indeed, as translating Jewish "emancipation" from its original socio-legal and political environments into a sonic-artistic one, aesthetically empowering the nonharmonious element that Jewish existence stood for.³³

HaCohen goes on to make the point that Schoenberg had a particular interest, including through his paintings, in "the 'dou-

---

31 Wagner, *Das Judenthum in der Musik*, 26.
32 Julie Brown, "Schoenberg's Early Wagnerisms: Atonality and the Redemption of Ahasuerus," *Cambridge Opera Journal* 6, no. 1 (1994): 60.
33 Ruth HaCohen, *The Music Libel against the Jews* (New Haven: Yale University Press, 2011), 288–89.

bling, dividing and interchanging of the self' — the heart of the *Unheimlich*, according to Freud."[34] In parallel fashion, Schoenberg's use of *Sprechstimme* "upset the exclusivity of the musical over the general sonic, opening it up for other kinds of 'indiscrete' sound — mechanical, urban, and the like."[35] As Harold Innis has noted, "the spoken word was in its origins a half-way house between singing and speech, an outlet for intense feelings rather than intelligible expression."[36] Relatedly, the twelve-tone system "emerged from within an oratorical environment,"[37] and, in the light of HaCohen's analysis, Schoenberg's emphasis on voice can be understood as invoking the Temple as a place of oral prayer via an architecture of "frozen music,"[38] his twelve-tone system, with the goal of restoring psalmodic culture to the People of the Book.[39]

HaCohen's thesis has a mediatic context that resonates significantly with the history of musicology. As Gary Tomlinson has argued, song was the "fundamental category" of musical understanding before the 18th century rise of musicological

---

34 Ibid., 290, internal quote from Freud's essay on the uncanny.
35 Ibid., 292.
36 Harold Adams Innis, *Empire and Communications* (Oxford: Clarendon Press, 1950), 9.
37 HaCohen, *The Music Libel against the Jews*, 298. Schoenberg's mother came from a family of cantors. See Bojan Bujić, *Arnold Schoenberg* (London: Phaidon, 2011), 14.
38 The notion that "architecture is frozen music" is attributed to Goethe in the *Conversations with Eckerman,* trans. Margaret Fuller (London: Hilliard, Gray, 1839), 282.
39 As Richard Taruskin writes, "antiphonal psalmody implied the use of two choirs answering each to each, as most famously described in the high priest Nehemiah's account of the dedication of the Jerusalem walls in 445 BCE, when vast choirs (and orchestras!) mounted the walls on opposite sides of the city gates and made a joyful noise unto the Lord. The verse structure of the psalms themselves, consisting of paired hemistichs, half-lines that state a single thought in different words [...] suggests that antiphony was their original mode of performance." See the section on "The Origins of Gregorian Chant" in chapter 1, "The Curtain Goes Up," *The Oxford History of Western Music,* at http://www.oxfordwesternmusic.com. See also Erich Werner, *The Sacred Bridge: Liturgical Parallels in Synagogue and Early Church* (London: Dobson, 1959).

studies.[40] It was posited as a phenomenon "shared by Europe with the rest of the world. [...] [T]he singing of non-Europeans was not differentiated in any categorical way from European song,"[41] a point of particular importance in the context of the music libel of the Jews. By the 18th century, however, a divide emerged: song was considered to be characteristic of primitive cultures, and "music" of civilized, European cultures. "If around 1700 song had offered a conceptual umbrella under which the world's musical activities, non-European and European, might gather (if uneasily), now instrumental music—music without words, *nonsong*—posed a new, exclusionary category redolent of European spiritual superiority."[42] This shift hinged on the notion (as expressed by Nikolaus Forkel's *Allgemeine Geschichte der Musik* of 1788) that "music progresses not only in tandem with language but also with writing."[43] In effect, the shift from song to music adumbrates the shift from orality to literacy.

---

40 Gary Tomlinson, "Musicology, Anthropology, History," in *The Cultural Study of Music*, ed. Martin Clayton et al. (New York: Routledge, 2003), 31–44.
41 Ibid., 33.
42 Ibid., 34.
43 Ibid., 36.

five

While Schoenberg's musical career has a profound political aspect, the political element in Gould's work is less obvious, and oriented nationally rather than internationally via the series of three radio documentaries about Canada that he conceived of as musical compositions: *The Idea of North, The Latecomers,* and *The Quiet in the Land.* Gould referred to these documentaries as his "so-called 'Solitude Trilogy'" in which he explores "the political dimension of isolation."[1] The documentaries seek to articulate the possibility of a *polis* not bound by existing political structures. *The Idea of North,* produced in the Canadian centennial year of 1967, has had massive cultural resonance in Canada, in many cases being taken as a metaphor of the nation itself. The assumption that Gould was celebrating Canada as a "northern" nation ignores, however, the complexities of the work, especially its overriding sense of irony — among the opening words are "I don't go for this northmanship bit at all."[2] Gould consistently undermines nationalist notions of belonging in these documentaries and substitutes kinship models for them. As he stated in

---

1   Gould to John Fraser, July 4, 1978, in John P.L. Roberts and Ghyslaine Guertin, eds., *Glenn Gould: Selected Letters* (Toronto: Oxford University Press, 1992), 237.
2   *Glenn Gould's Solitude Trilogy: Three Sound Documentaries* (Toronto: CBC, 1992), 3 CDs, PSCD 2003-3.

an interview with Ulla Colgrass, when asked what he thought about Canadian nationalism, "I think it is rather silly, I really haven't much sympathy with barriers."[3] Gould conceived of the documentaries in terms of "counterpoint," of "ternary form, as one would think of it in music," of "a kind of trio sonata texture," "a kind of Webern-like continuity-in-crossover," a "passacaglia of fact,"[4] all of which reflect the political ambiguities of the trilogy. In conceiving of his works in musical terms, Gould sought to avoid the production of documentaries which, "to borrow Mr. McLuhan's term" sounded "linear,"[5] a notion he put to the test as well in his 1974 documentary on that most non-linear of composers, Arnold Schoenberg.

The "solitude trilogy" indirectly raises the issue of Gould's reclusiveness, which has become one of the great shibboleths of his career: much more commentary has been made about this quality of his lifestyle than of his performance practices. Mark Kingwell puts it precisely: "lacking one Gould" — the Gould who recused himself from public performance — "the public generates multiple ones, a succession of Gould-ghosts, all of them vaporous and partial"[6] in its attempt to make sense of a life lived outside the bounds of conformity. Yet the "reclusive" Gould had many friends, interacted with scores of CBC producers and technicians over several decades, was outgoing enough to visit McLuhan at his University of Toronto office and his Wells Hill Avenue home, wrote hundreds of letters, talked for hours on the telephone, enjoyed a number of performative identities, had one major love affair and many minor ones, and drew more than 3,000 people to his memorial service in 1982. "To live

---

3 Gould, interview with Ulla Colgrass, in John P.L. Roberts, ed., *The Art of Glenn Gould* (Toronto: Malcolm Lester Books, 1999), 351.
4 Glenn Gould, *The Glenn Gould Reader*, ed. Tim Page (Toronto: Lester & Orpen Dennys, 1984), 375, 378, 379, 388.
5 Ibid., 374.
6 Mark Kingwell, *Glenn Gould* (Toronto: Penguin, 2009), 6. Michel Schneider has remarked that "There is something repugnant and unjust in the canonisation of Gould after his death," in *Glenn Gould Piano Solo* (Paris: Gallimard, 1988), 143, my trans.

without living," asked Georges Leroux about Gould's lifestyle, "is that still living? Or is it another kind of life?"[7] In some ways anticipating the Internet era, when we have electronic "friends," thanks to Facebook and email, Gould more pointedly was structuring his life outside the norms dictated by conventional societal roles, just as he had sought to articulate his performance practices away from the concert hall and his notion of belonging outside nationalism. He experienced his being relationally, with a conviction and inner purpose that characterizes his achievements as a whole. Gould played on this performatively, with his multiple identities, from Herbert von Hochmeister to Dr. Karlheinz Klopweisser and Sir Nigel Twitt-Thornwaite. Here we begin to glimpse another aspect of Gouldian politics, which were decidedly personal and sought to undermine the typecasting that Gould associated with concert performing. In the studio he could be performer, composer, and conductor at the same time.

Very little of this political orientation, however defined, enters into Gould's commentaries on Schoenberg. For Gould, the music was an exercise in abstraction,[8] although Gould does write at one point that "in the very year when Schoenberg, in exile, was writing his most vehement protests about war in general, and Hitler's in particular, Strauss was concocting, for the Munich operas[,] the gentlest and most disengaged of all his theatrical works, *Capriccio*."[9] Nevertheless, Gould tends to demonstrate an insensitivity to Schoenberg's personal/political context, although this was not unique to Gould; as Erhard Bahr has observed, Mann's *Dr. Faustus* displays "a Germany without anti-Semitism."[10] But Gould's position does reflect his Canadi-

---

7   George Leroux, *Partita for Glenn Gould,* trans. Donald Winkler (Montreal: McGill-Queens University Press, 2010) 4.
8   In *Arnold Schoenberg: A Perspective* (Cincinatti: University of Cincinnati, 1964), Gould writes that "music is always abstract" (8).
9   Gould to Peter Symcox, December 10, 1972, in Roberts and Guertin, *Selected Letters,* 187.
10 Erhard Bahr, *Weimar on the Pacific* (Berkeley: University of California Press, 2007) 250. This is particularly odd in the context of Mann's wartime broadcasts, published as *Deutsche Hörer!* in 1942 with editions following until 1945.

anness. Canada has traditionally thought of itself as a nation in which geography overwhelms history — and this in a nation in which Indigenous cultures can claim a historical continuity of circa 15,000 years. However, it is legitimate to state that Gould, like Schoenberg, was concerned with opening up new spaces, musically and culturally and politically. They did this — Gould exclusively and Schoenberg transitionally — in the "new world," which recontextualized music from national(ist) expression to post-national and postmodern production, from historical "progression" to postmodern simultaneity. The nation that was the subject of Gould's musings suffered from a permanent identity crisis — a "borderline case,"[11] as McLuhan once put it. The nation that Schoenberg alluded to in *Moses und Aron* was as much Zion as Israel, and Judaism was a nation outside national borders — even after the founding of the state of Israel.

---

11 Marshall McLuhan, "Canada: The Borderline Case," in *The Canadian Imagination,* ed. David Staines (Cambridge: Harvard University Press, 1977), 226–48.

six

Gould's study of Schoenberg's music was deeply influenced by René Leibowitz's *Schoenberg and His School: The Contemporary State of the Language of Music*,[1] a book which the young Gould memorized.[2] Section one of the book is dedicated to Jean-Paul Sartre[3] and Simone de Beauvoir, and the introduction makes reference to Heidegger's notion of *Entwurf*, or "pro-ject," which, Leibowitz writes, means that "by existing[,] the human body *pro-jects* its world, causes the world to *be there*."[4] To this sense that one is thrown into the world, one responds through *Stimmung*, a becoming attuned (in the sense of musical pitch) to one's being in the world, which is the essence of one's freedom.[5]

---

1   René Leibowitz, *Schoenberg and His School: The Contemporary State of the Language of Music*, trans. Dika Newlin (New York: Da Capo, 1949). Gould recommends the book highly in a letter to Christian Geelhaar, December 16, 1959, in John P.L. Roberts and Ghyslaine Guertin, eds., *Glenn Gould: Selected Letters* (Toronto: Oxford University Press, 1992), 23.
2   Kevin Bazzana, *Wondrous Strange: The Life and Art of Glenn Gould* (Toronto: McClelland and Stewart, 2003), 91.
3   On Sartre as pianist see François Noudelmann, *The Philosopher's Touch: Sartre, Nietzsche and Barthes at the Piano*, trans. Brian J. Reilly (Columbia: Columbia University Press, 2012).
4   Leibowitz, *Schoenberg and His School*, xxi.
5   See Simon Critchley, "Being and Time Part 4: Thrown into this World," *The Guardian*, June 29, 2009, http://www.theguardian.com/

It was this engaged, processual aspect of Schoenberg's music that Leibowitz wanted to communicate. Both a student of Schoenberg, as well as a performer of his work,[6] Leibowitz's was the first study of Schoenberg, and focused on "a rational examination of his serial procedure."[7] This focus had a significant influence on subsequent studies of Schoenberg, even though it was "contrary to Leibowitz's intentions, for he had wanted to communicate his enthusiasm for the music of the Vienna School[,] with the analytical aspect as his means and not an end in itself."[8] But even if a misunderstanding of Leibowitz's intentions, the notion of Schoenberg as an unremitting formalist remained, and had a deep influence on Gould, who was either blind to the political context of Schoenberg's life and work or chose to ignore it as not relevant to Schoenberg's music.

Another writer on Schoenberg who influenced Gould was Theodor Wiesengrund Adorno. Gould encountered Adorno via *Prisms,* originally published in 1955, which includes a laudatory essay on Schoenberg that Adorno wrote after the composer's death. In his copy of *Prisms,* Gould highlighted Adorno's opening comment that Schoenberg's music demands of the listener

---

    commentisfree/belief/2009/jun/29/religion-philosophy. On the connections among the morpheme *stim* in Heidegger's philosophy see Herman Philipse, *Heidegger's Philosophy of Being: A Critical Interpretation* (Princeton: Princeton University Press, 2001), who writes that through "the common morpheme *stim* in *Stimmung* (mood), *Stimme* (voice), *stimmen* (to tune, to be correct), *abstimmen* (to tune in on), *bestimmen* (to determine), and *Bestimmung* (purpose, destiny) [...] Heidegger suggests [...] that Being, by its soundless voice (*lautlose Stimme*), determines (*bestimmen*) us in our destiny (*Bestimmung*), and that we experience this determination in fundamental moods (*Stimmungen*), which tune us in on (*stimmen, abstimmen*) what is. Moods, according to the later Heidegger, are fundamental because they tune us in (*stimmen*) on the voice (*Stimme*) of Being" (232).

6 H.H. Stuckenschmidt, *Schoenberg: His Life, World, and Work,* trans. Humphrey Searle (London: Calder, 1977), 349.

7 Bojan Bujić, *Arnold Schoenberg* (London: Phaidon, 2011), 214.

8 Ibid.

"not mere contemplation but praxis,"⁹ and Gould extended this concept to his own performance/compositions. Like Leibowitz, Adorno (who studied composition with Schoenberg's student Alban Berg) proclaimed Schoenberg the epitome of modernism in music while critiquing "mechanical"[10] aspects of the twelve-tone system. Adorno's vacillation about Schoenberg's music is reflected in Mann's *Doctor Faustus,* on which Adorno "advised" the author (appearing in the novel as "Wiesengrund"[11]). Schoenberg also occupies a prominent place in Adorno's *Philosophy of New Music* (1949), written when Adorno, like Schoenberg, was living in Los Angeles. Adorno asserts there that "the musical substance of Schoenberg may well one day prove superior to Wagner's."[12] The context for this remark, and Adorno's central concern in the book, is "the subsumption of music to commercialized mass production,"[13] epitomized by popular music and jazz, although Stravinsky comes in for major criticism, in that his music is deemed by Adorno to be recidivist, rather than progressive. (The section on Schoenberg is titled "Schoenberg and Progress.") If the modernist trend in music was a reaction to the debasement of music by the culture industry, the battle has (post WW2) been lost, Adorno implies; "calculated idiocy" now reigns via "unprincipled intellectual compliancy" in composers such as Benjamin Britten and his "pretentious meagerness," and in Elgar's "trumped-up fame," all of it characterized by "a taste for bad taste" constituting a collective "rubbish heap."[14] "The numerically small group of connoisseurs was displaced by all those who could afford the price of a ticket and wanted to prove

---

9   Theodor W. Adorno, *Prisms,* trans. Samuel and Sherry Weber (Cambridge: MIT Press, 1967), 150.
10 Bujić, *Arnold Schoenberg,* 123, 151.
11 Adrian Daub, "Introduction" to *The Doctor Faustus Dossier,* ed. E. Randol Schoenberg, trans. Adrian Feuchtwanger and Barbara Zeisl Schoenberg (Berkeley: University of California Press), 17–20.
12 Theodor W. Adorno, *Philosophy of New Music,* trans., ed. and with an intro. by Robert Hullot-Kenter (Minneapolis: University of Minnesota Press, 2004), 22.
13 Ibid., 3.
14 Ibid., 9–10.

to others that they were cultured"; "all that the public grasps of traditional music is its crudest aspects" as performed in "the vacuous ceremonial of the concert hall."[15] Because people's ears have been "inundated by light music,"[16] they no longer know how to listen. "Humanity in the age of omnipresent radios and gramophones has actually forgotten the experience of music,"[17] a comment which Adorno would extend to all media in an essay on "The Culture Industry."[18] The implication is clear: musical culture has declined in direct proportion to the rise of electronic media, which is surely ironic in the case of both Gould and Schoenberg, since the latter's career was inflected by the rise of recording, and the former's became purely a product of the recording studio after 1964. Yet Adorno's notion of a Schoenberg who was the austere manifestation of musical abstraction had a significant effect on the reception of Schoenberg's work, much greater than that of Leibowitz. As Bojan Bujić comments, "by attributing historical inevitability to everything Schoenberg did, Adorno unwittingly made the reception of his music more difficult,"[19] especially in a context in which music was increasingly mediated technologically. This was Kittler's critique of Adorno: "Amplifiers put philosophy out of commission. They cover up traditional musical values such as thematic workmanship or polyphonic style — all these fundamentally written data — and replace them with sound."[20] To speak productively of Schoenberg, Adorno required a *Medienphilosophie* which his stance toward media forbade him.

A more productive understanding of Schoenberg's music was proposed by R. Murray Schafer, a composer as well as a the-

---

15 Ibid., 11–12.
16 Ibid., 12.
17 Ibid., 21.
18 Theodor W. Adorno and Max Horkheimer, "The Culture Industry," in *Dialectic of Enlightenment*, trans. Edmund Jephcott (Stanford: Stanford University Press, 2002), 41–72.
19 Bujić, *Arnold Schoenberg*, 123.
20 Friedrich Kittler, "World-Breath: On Wagner's Media Technology," in *Opera through Other Eyes*, ed. David J. Levin (Stanford: Stanford University Press, 1994), 224.

orizer of the soundscape, who, like Gould, came powerfully under the influence of McLuhan in the 1960s. Schafer writes in *The Tuning of the World* that there are two Greek myths that speak of the origin of music. In one of these, Athena is said to have created a *nomos* — a melody used by the singers of epic — in honor of the sisters of Medusa, whose mourned the beheading of their sibling. In the other, Hermes is said to have invented the lyre when he realized that the shell of a turtle was resonant. As Schafer comments, "[i]n the first of these myths music arises as subjective emotion; in the second it arises with the discovery of sonic properties in the materials of the universe."[21] While the first myth represents music as Dionysian, the second articulates it as Apollonian, and it is this understanding of music that Schafer associates with Schoenberg: "[i]n the Apollonian view music is exact, serene, mathematical, associated with transcendental visions of Utopia and the Harmony of Spheres. [...] It is the basis of Pythagoras's speculations and those of the medieval theoreticians (where music was taught as a subject of the quadrivium, along with arithmetic, geometry, and astronomy), as well as Schoenberg's twelve-note method of composition. Its methods of exposition are number theories. It seeks to harmonize the world through acoustic design."[22] This serves to contextualize Schoenberg's musical and political aspirations in a way that Adorno, with his exclusive focus on musical "progress," fails to do, although Schoenberg more accurately acceded to Nietzsche's exhortation to worship at the alter of both Apollo and Dionysus.

---

21 R. Murray Schafer, *The Tuning of the World* (New York: Knopf, 1977), 6.
22 Ibid. Gould has been studied as an "Apollonian" artist in a famous profile by Joseph Roddy with that title, published in *The New Yorker*, May 14, 1960. "Schönberg" is mentioned once, as representative of "the tone-row systematizers" (74). Roddy notes that H.H. Stuckenschmidt, the biographer of Schoenberg and "Germany's most respected music critic," called Gould "the greatest pianist since Ferruccio Busoni" (89) after hearing him perform with Herbert von Karajan and the Berlin Philharmonic.

seven

Among Gould's many works devoted to Schoenberg was his one book, *Arnold Schoenberg: A Perspective* (with its André Masson portrait of Schoenberg on the cover), five essays now reprinted in *The Glenn Gould Reader* (which also includes the text of the Schoenberg book), an essay written in grade 13 in defense of the Schoenberg school, a 1951 lecture (his first) at the Royal Conservatory of Music in Toronto delivered on the occasion of Schoenberg's death, a 1953 analysis, also read at the Conservatory, of Schoenberg's *Piano Concerto* ("of which he gave the Canadian première a few days later"[1]), a lecture on the Schoenberg school given on his 1957 Russian tour (when such musicians were proscribed in the Soviet Union),[2] a radio documentary, *Arnold Schoenberg: The Man Who Changed Music,* that aired on CBC in 1962, a television program co-produced by the CBC and

---

1   Kevin Bazzana, *Wondrous Strange: The Life and Art of Glenn Gould* (Toronto: McClelland and Stewart, 2003), 110.
2   Gould's concert tour of Moscow and Leningrad in 1957 was the first such tour by a North American pianist. The tour took political courage at a time when composers such as Schoenberg were branded as decadent. See James K. Wright, "Glenn Gould, Arnold Schoenberg, and Soviet Reception of the Second Viennese School," in *Schoenberg's Chamber Music, Schoenberg's World,* eds. Wright and Allan M. Gillmor (Hillsdale: Pendragon Press, 2009), 237–58.

the BBC in 1966, and a 10-week radio series on Schoenberg that was broadcast in 1974 (with the text published in French translation as *La série Schönberg*).

Arnold Schoenberg: A Perspective was published in 1964, the year that Gould retired from the stage, and further links that retirement to the role that Schoenberg played in Gould's musical career. In his foreword to the book, Arthur Darack notes that Gould makes the "bold historical judgment that Schoenberg represents simplicity, despite the common, labored charge of undue, artificial complexity."[3] In fact, Darack continues, "Gould's analysis, comparing [Schoenberg] to Monteverdi, [...] places him in the mainstream as a great historic synthesizer and simplifier."[4] This comparison is particularly Gouldian in its audaciousness. It could mean simply (as Darack suggests) that both Monteverdi and Schoenberg were active at turning points in musical history, or (again, according to Darack), that "the chromatic scale had to be systematized."[5] Darack quotes Manfred Bukofzer's *Music in the Baroque Era* to the effect that Monteverdi was "'conservative with regard to the preservation of polyphony in principle but revolutionary with regard to its transformation in practice.'"[6] Thus, "the chaconne bass of Monteverdi [...] had a function not completely remote from the 'tone row' of Schoenberg."[7] What emerges from this analysis is Darack's understanding that Gould refused to consider Schoenberg a musical outlier; Gould's Schoenberg is very much to be understood as part of the musical tradition.

Gould argues, rather, that Schoenberg's career can be understood in terms of his acceptance of, rejection of, and reconciliation with the musical tradition.[8] This implies, as Gould notes, a rejection of musical evolution, a point Gould also makes with

---

3   Arthur Darack, "Foreword," to Glenn Gould, *Arnold Schoenberg: A Perspective* (Cincinnati: University of Cincinnati Press, 1964), vi.
4   Ibid.
5   Ibid.
6   Ibid., vii.
7   Ibid.
8   Gould, *Arnold Schoenberg*, 1.

reference to the career of Richard Strauss, whose last works are "hopelessly old-fashioned."[9] Gould states that Schoenberg appeared on the musical scene when the revolution put in place during the Renaissance shift from the modal to the tonal was being reversed, a position that somewhat reflects McLuhan's thesis that electronic media were reversing 500 years of print culture, resulting in a return to acoustic space. Gould's most compelling argument in *Arnold Schoenberg*, however, comes at the end, when he contemplates the legacy of Schoenberg's musical compositions. While there is no Schoenberg "school," Gould makes the intriguing suggestion that atonality has come to characterize our soundscape, and is now integrated into our listening environment by everything from contemporary opera to movie soundtracks to TV shows, all of which have served to make "a dissonant vocabulary [...] perfectly comprehensible."[10] Gould had a very clear understanding that this environment was the one created by electronic media; as he put it in a letter written in 1976, "in the past few decades, we have witnessed the creation of that network which now, quite literally, encompasses the earth."[11]

This concept of a musical environment produced via electronic media was the governing one in Gould's 10 part radio documentary on Schoenberg, aired on the CBC in 1974. As was typical in Gould documentaries, the pianist wrote both the interviewer's questions (Ken Haslam, in this case), and his own responses. The full text of the documentary (as opposed to the text transmitted, which contained cuts) has been published as *La série Schönberg*,[12] edited by Ghyslaine Guertin. Guertin argues in her introduction that Gould devoted so much attention to Schoenberg because he recognized himself in the composer, such that the documentary sketches out a self-portrait. The traits

---

9   Ibid., 2.
10 Ibid., 18.
11 John P.L. Roberts and Ghyslaine Guertin, eds., *Glenn Gould: Selected Letters* (Toronto: Oxford University Press, 1992), 233.
12 Glenn Gould, *La série Schönberg*, ed. Ghyslaine Guertin (Paris: Christian Bourgois, 1998).

that Gould recognized that he had in common with Schoenberg were anti-conformism, and the fact that both he and Schoenberg were autodidacts, Gould in musicology and Schoenberg in composition. Despite these similarities, Gould was not uncritical in his assessment of Schoenberg; it was not serialism that made Schoenberg great, he argued, but what Schoenberg made of serialism that was important.

At the beginning of the documentary, Gould demarcates the central paradox of Schoenberg's career: his fundamental importance to 20th century music, and his lack of popularity as a composer. He remarks that Schoenberg's music remains "among the most passionate and intense"[13] that he has experienced, especially the *Lieder* that Schoenberg wrote early in his career (such as *Waldsonne*). Paradoxically, this music is rarely performed, unlike, for example, Alban Berg's *Seven Songs of Youth*. Gould advances the theory that Schoenberg's *Lieder* are under-represented in the repertory because the relationship between piano and singer is atypical. Whereas in other *Lieder*, the piano takes a subservient role to the singer, in Schoenberg the pianist's role is equal to that of the singer. This theory is remarkable, in that it extends to performance practice the notion central to twelve-tone composing that all notes are equal, suggesting thereby that the importance of the twelve-tone system is not "only" musical but also that it constitutes a poetics. As Schoenberg insisted, "my works are twelve-note *compositions,* not *twelve-note* compositions."[14]

In his discussion of *Sprechstimme,* Gould states that he has only recently recorded some excerpts from *Pierrot Lunaire* for television (with Patricia Rideout performing the vocals), and that he finds the technique hard to digest. Gould acknowledges, however, that the technique was one of Schoenberg's major achievements, suggesting that Schoenberg had "a superb sense

---

13 Ibid., my trans. throughout.
14 Schoenberg to Rudolf Kolisch, July 27, 1932, in Arnold Schoenberg, *Arnold Schoenberg Letters,* ed. Erwin Stein, trans. Eithne Wilkins and Ernst Kaiser (New York: St. Martin's Press, 1965), 164–65.

of vocal inflections,"[15] as is evident, as well, from the *Lieder* he composed. What Gould particularly notes is the "aleatory"[16] aspect of *Sprechstimme*, a quality which has connections to John Cage's performance practices. Cage figures in the last part of the documentary, Gould having interviewed him via telephone; in the following dialogue from the documentary, both parts have been written by Gould:

> KEN HASLAM: Cage was one of the major proponents of free improvisation ...
> GLENN GOULD: Of aleatory music, yes, absolutely...
> KH: And also of electronic music, wasn't he?
> GG: Yes, and this was well before recording technology became accessible. [...] And in the fifties, he had programmed [...] the first *happenings*. In fact, his quasi astrological music using the *I Ching* of more recent years is a sort of extended *happening*, isn't it?
> KH: Yes, but all of these Cagean innovations are related to, in some way or another, [...] his fascination for — how can one say this — his fascination with noise for noise's sake, isn't that so?
> GG: More or less, yes.
> KH: OK, then let me repeat: I am simply unable to understand how a musician who had...
> GG: Rather anarchical ideas?
> KH: Exactly! I am unable to understand how such a musician decided to work with someone like Schoenberg. Despite all his own efforts at innovation, he was a veritable traditionalist both in terms of his music and his respect for the past. It is this that I've learned from our discussions for this series.
> GG: I agree with you, Ken. It is truly curious that Cage decided to study with Schoenberg, and, as I said, the interview surprised me as well. I was of course expecting to find in Cage a highly tolerant person, and thus his way of defending

---

15 Gould, *La série Schoenberg*, 74.
16 Ibid.

the music of Schoenberg didn't surprise me, since this was part of his "live and let live" philosophy. But I wasn't at all expecting to hear him make such a sympathetic judgment on Schoenberg's historical position. In my opinion, this sympathy is revelatory. Cage is probably — and one can say this with complete equanimity — the one American composer to have had a certain influence on the European musical scene. I don't mean to suggest that he is the only composer to have been appreciated there or admired for his way of doing things ...

KH: But the only one to have been considered as a sort of guru.

GG: Exactly. [...] [W]hat was most important were his reflections on the idea of sound and music. He extolled in this domain an overlapping of Western and Eastern philosophies. In brief, if the European scene learned anything from him, it was from his ideas as much as from his music itself.

KH: Exactly, yes. Because didn't he write a work, if one is able to use that word, entirely constructed of silence?

GG: Even I'm unsure if the word "work" is appropriate here. But he did write a work called *Four Minutes and Thirty-Three Seconds*. [...] But even in his works composed in order to be, to a certain extent, heard, rather than to be an occasion for reflection, Cage was less interested in creating musical works than in launching "probes," as Mr. McLuhan might put it.[17]

Might this be said of Gould as well? As Kevin Bazzana has asserted, "Gould often sounded surprisingly like another contemporary devotee of McLuhan: John Cage."[18] But what is most fascinating about this "dialogue" is Gould's suggestion of a Schoenbergian influence being exercised through Cage which takes the form of a melding of Eastern and Western forms, and

---

17 Ibid., 175–76.
18 Kevin Bazzana, *Glenn Gould: The Performer in the Work* (Oxford: Clarendon Press, 1997), 74.

that Schoenberg's influence extends beyond the musical domain via a poetics of composition.

eight

Cage was arguably one of Schoenberg's most important students ("an inventor — of genius"¹ was Schoenberg's assessment), not because he followed in Schoenberg's twelve-tone footsteps (like Berg and Webern) but through the importance he placed on the environmental dimension of music in the era of the technological reproduction of sound. In "The Future of Music: Credo," a talk given in Seattle in 1937, Cage stated that "NEW METHODS WILL BE DISCOVERED, BEARING A DEFINITE RELATION TO SCHOENBERG'S TWELVE-TONE SYSTEM. Schoenberg's method assigns to each material, in a group of equal materials, its function with respect to the group."² Like Gould, Cage understood the twelve-tone system to be a poetics, a mode of artistic production, rather than a mode of composition strictly tied to music. As Gould discovered in his interview, Cage maintained his allegiance to Schoenberg's poetics throughout his career; late in life, Cage stated that as a young man he was "like a tiger in de-

---

1   Schoenberg, quoted by Thomas S. Hines, "'Then Not Yet "Cage"': The Los Angeles Years, 1912–1938," in *John Cage: Composed in America,* eds. Marjorie Perloff and Charles Junkerman (Chicago: University of Chicago Press, 1994), 93.
2   John Cage, "Credo," in *Sound by Artists,* eds. Dan Lander and Micah Lexier (Toronto: Art Metropole, 1990), 17.

fense of Schoenberg."[3] Schoenberg had told Cage that "without a feeling for harmony [he] would always encounter an obstacle, a wall through which he wouldn't be able to pass. My reply [said Cage] was that in that case I would devote my life to beating my head against that wall — and maybe that is what I've been doing ever since."[4] Once again, this suggests we must reassess Schoenberg's influence such that it extends beyond musical composition. Schoenberg was a synaesthetic artist, producing not only musical compositions but visual art works (and technological inventions, such as his music typewriter). In moving musical composition from a temporal axis (the ultimate expression of which in Schoenberg's musical context was Wagner's *Liebestod*) to a spatial one, and affirming thus that artistic meaning was a product not only of temporal progression but spatial juxtaposition,[5] Schoenberg inaugurated a modernism that was as powerful as Einstein's theorization of spacetime relativity. If we understand the composer's achievement in this larger context, then we are presented with a much broader legacy: Schoenberg as teacher — and what he taught us was to understand art beyond the closure of traditional modes of production, to understand being as beyond individuality, to understand politics as beyond traditional boundaries. In 1991, John Ashbery said of his own avowedly difficult poetry that one way of reading it "was to think of it as music": "[w]hat you hear at a given moment is a refraction of what's gone before or after."[6] While living in New York, Ashbery had encountered the work of John Cage, "whose atonal compositions had a lasting influence on him."[7] When one recalls that McLuhan and Cage often met at Cage's New York

---

3 Hines "Then Not Yet 'Cage,'" 92.
4 Ibid.
5 Schoenberg writes about mastering "the difficulties of condensation and juxtaposition" in "A Self-Analysis" (1948), included in *Style and Idea: Selected Writings of Arnold Schoenberg*, ed. Leonard Stein, trans. Leo Black (Berkeley: University of California Press, 1984), 78.
6 Quoted by David Orr and Dinitia Smith in "Pulitzer-Winning Poetic Voice Often Echoed, Never Matched," *The New York Times*, September 4, 2017, A1, A16.
7 Ibid.

apartment,[8] and that McLuhan was the mentor of Gould, and that Ashbery, like Schoenberg, was attuned as much to music as to the visual arts, then the circle of Schoenberg's influence and legacy expands exponentially.

Schoenberg's influence is clearly present in contemporary "new music"; its performative aspects overlap, as well, with composed theatre, which claims Schoenberg as a forbearer. At the World New Music Days (convened by the International Society for New Music,[9] Canadian Section) held in Vancouver, Canada, in November 2017,[10] the overriding characteristics the compositions had in common were playful dissonance, performativity, the use of electronic media, post-instrumentality, and juxtapositional rather than linear forms. In one presentation, of circa thirty contemporary pieces for piano, the instrument was often used in conjunction with an iPod (to produce sinewaves), or as a sounding board. There was little use of the keyboard in piano compositions by an international group of composers, including Judith Weir, Chiyoko Szlavnics, Heera Kim, and David Brynjar Franzson. Other pieces magnified the sound of plastic cups being crumpled, or a sewing machine in operation. These are clearly Cagean resonances, but they are Cage via the Schoenberg who liberated Cage from the tonal imperative. As Charles Rosen has put it, "the later Schoenberg became a model followed so many times that we hear him most often without being aware of it."[11]

The argument that Schoenberg is very important but little-performed ultimately bears no weight in this context. James Joyce was as important to literary modernism as Schoenberg was to musical modernism, yet *Finnegans Wake* is little read or taught. The same could be said about Gertrude Stein and many

---

8   See Richard Cavell, *Remediating McLuhan* (Amsterdam: Amsterdam University Press, 2016), 166–67n6.

9   Schoenberg was made Honorary President of the ISCM after WW2. See Bojan Bujić, *Arnold Schoenberg* (London: Phaidon: 2011), 204.

10 The series was produced by David Pay, Artistic Director of Vancouver's Music on Main, http://www.musiconmain.ca.

11 Charles Rosen, *Schoenberg* (London: Fontana, 1976), 21.

other modernist authors. Their work, however, has not been superseded. As T.S. Eliot (another modernist author) stated in "Tradition and the Individual Talent" (1919), the work of a new artist changes the entire system of artistic expression; it does not represent an evolutionary singularity.[12] Furthermore, media produce their effects differently, some in "low definition" (which is involving and process-oriented) and others in "high definition" (not inviting deep engagement)[13] and therefore our encounters with them as listeners or viewers will be different. And the remediation of music, literature, and the visual arts by the Internet (such that it is possible to speak of "post-Internet art")[14] reconfigures these effects again. On YouTube, Schoenberg's *Suite* (op. 29, Boulez conducting) has been listened to more than 17,000 times; Hilary Hahn's performance of the *Violin Concerto* (op. 36) has been viewed over 100,000 times on various sites; and Maurizio Pollini's performance of the *Three Piano Pieces* (op. 11) has been listened to 120,000 times (as of December 2017). Clearly, the concert hall performance is not the only yardstick or perhaps even the major one, now, for assessing the performance life of an artist's work.

The theater is now increasingly ranged beside the concert hall as a place where performances structured according to musical principles take place; relatedly, the art gallery is increasing-

---

12 "[W]hat happens when a new work of art is created is something that happens simultaneously to all the works of art which preceded it. The existing monuments form an ideal order among themselves, which is modified by the introduction of the new (the really new) work of art among them. The existing order is complete before the new work arrives; for order to persist after the supervention of novelty, the whole existing order must be, if ever so slightly, altered; and so the relations, proportions, values of each work of art toward the whole are readjusted; and this is conformity between the old and the new." See T.S. Eliot, "Tradition and the Individual Talent," *Egoist* (September and November, 1919), http://tseliot.com/essays/tradition-and-the-individual-talent.

13 This is McLuhan's theory of hot and cool media, as elaborated in *Understanding Media: The Extensions of Man* (New York: McGraw-Hill, 1964), 22–32.

14 See, for example, Lauren Cornell and Ed Halter, eds., *Mass Effect: Art and the Internet in the Twenty-First Century* (Cambridge: MIT Press), 2015.

ly home to sound installations. "Composed theater," one such mode of theatrical performance, places Schoenberg among its forbearers. As David Roesner writes in *Composed Theatre: Aesthetics, Practices, Processes,*

> [s]ince the beginning of the twentieth century, it has been an ongoing interest of composers like Arnold Schoenberg, John Cage, Mauricio Kagel, George Aperghis, Dieter Schnebel, Hans-Joachim Hespos, Manos Tsangaris, Charlotte Seither and Heiner Goebbels — to name but a few — to approach the theatrical stage and its means of expression as *musical* material. They treat voice, gesture, movement, light, sound, image, design and other features of theatrical production according to musical principles and compositional techniques and apply musical thinking to performance as a whole. This idea is again flourishing among composers, directors and theatre collectives, as reflected in recent developments towards postdramatic forms that de-emphasize text, narrative and fictional characters, seeking alternative dramaturgies (visual, spatial, temporal, musical), and focusing on the sonic and visual materialities of the stage and the performativity of their material components.[15]

Roesner goes on to note that, concurrently, "musical composition has increasingly expanded its range of 'instruments' to include live video, lighting design, live sound electronics, costumes and spatial arrangements, and has paid closer attention to the theatricality of the musical performer."[16] Particularly influential on the poetics of composed theater have been Schoenberg's comments about his 1913 composition *Die glückliche Hand* that he was "*making music with the media of the stage* [*mit*

---

15 David Roesner, "Introduction: Composed Theatre in Context," in *Composed Theatre: Aesthetics, Practices, Processes,* eds. Matthias Rebstock and David Roesner (Bristol: Intellect, 2012), 10.

16 Ibid.

den Mitteln der Bühne musizieren],"[17] such that lights, music, acting, and staging were all coordinated. These theatrical poetics[18] reflect the dethroning of language that was a concomitant of theatrical modernism and the associated crisis in narrative: linearity was no longer deemed an adequate way of addressing the complexities of modern life, and, in the musical context, the Wagnerian model of narrative employed in his "music dramas" was rejected. As Schoenberg puts it, "[i]n Wagner's music-drama, he placed the drama in the foreground, whereas he had a supporting role in mind for the music."[19] To the static model of the *Gesamtkunstwerk*, Schoenberg proposes a process model in which "'it is every single word, every gesture, every beam of light, every costume and every image that does it: nothing should symbolize something other than what sounds usually symbolize. Everything should mean nothing less than the sounding notes mean.'"[20]

Matthias Rebstock claims that

---

17 Arnold Schoenberg, "Breslau lecture on *Die glückliche Hand*," in *Arnold Schoenberg / Wassily Kandinsky: Letters, Pictures and Documents,* ed. Jelena Hahl-Koch, trans. John C. Crawford (London: Faber and Faber, 1984), 105, emphasis in original.

18 Richard Taruskin polemicizes against the "poietic fallacy" in that it diverts the focus of musical understanding from the listener to the composer. My use of the term "poetics" is somewhat different, in its suggestion that Schoenberg's compositional method constituted a paradigm that has a larger application than to musical production alone. As such, my use of the term is also different from that employed by Carl Dahlhuas as summarized by John Covach in "Schoenberg's 'Poetics of Music,' the Twelve-Tone Method, and the Musical Idea," in *Schoenberg and Words: The Modernist Years,* eds. Charlotte M. Cross and Russell A. Berman (New York: Garland, 2000), 309–46. See Taruskin's "The Poietic Fallacy," *Musical Times* 145 (2004): 7–34. For a response, see Joseph Auner, "Composing on Stage: Schoenberg and the Creative Process as Public Per-formance," *19th Century Music* 29, no. 1 (2005): 64–93, especially the last section, "Poiesis R Us" (90–93).

19 Arnold Schoenberg, *Style and Idea Selected Writings,* ed. Leonard Stein (Berkeley: University of California Press, 1984), 105.

20 Quoted by Matthias Rebstock, "Composed Theatre: Mapping the Field," in Roesner and Rebstock, *Composed Theatre,* 31.

there are some features within the compositional bias of serial music that have become highly relevant for Composed Theatre. [...] [I]t was the clash of this highly organized structural music with the aesthetics of John Cage and the early happenings that unleashed enormous productivity in the field of music-theatre in the sixties, making this period the true starting point of Composed Theatre."[21]

As a method, seriality was independent of specific material, allowing it to be applied to any material that might form part of the theatrical performance. Thus, "following the internal logic of serial music, European composers finally arrived at a point quite similar to one that Cage had already made in the early fifties, even if on the basis of completely different aesthetic beliefs, when he sustained that virtually everything could turn into musical material."[22] Music at this point became truly environmental in its embrace of a post-literate acoustic space.

---

21 Ibid., 36.
22 Ibid.

nine

A key theorization of the postwar move toward acoustic space was Karlheinz Stockhausen's 1959 essay "Musik und Raum" ("Music and Space"), in which the composer "depicts the development of electronic music as an immediate consequence of the principle of equality of all musical parameters."[1] Schoenberg

---

1   Matthias Rebstock, "Composed Theatre: Mapping the Field," in *Composed Theatre: Aesthetics, Practices, Processes,* eds. Matthias Rebstock and David Roesner (Bristol: Intellect, 2012), 37. Carola Nielinger-Vakil notes in her chapter "Towards Spatial Composition," in *Luigi Nono: A Composer in Context* (Cambridge: Cambridge University Press, 2015), 85–122, that Nono wrote to Stockhausen about "the extension of 'musical space' and the autonomous use of the visual and acoustic dimensions" in Schoenberg's work and she states that "the wish to create new spatial conditions for greater listening awareness [...] was motivated, in part, by Nono's ongoing interest in Schoenberg in addition to the most advanced technological possibilities in contemporary theatre and music theatre. *Die glückliche Hand* (1909–13) was of particular interest to Nono because of its independent use of the visual and acoustic dimensions" (88). With particular reference to Schoenberg's compositional practices, Nono remarks: "[i]ngeniously begun by Arnold Schoenberg, the concept of serial composition (instead of the tonal order, the function of which has now been exhausted), has undergone a consistent historical development and gradually expanded from the determination of melodic-thematic interval relationships to the determination of all parameters of the musical language. With it, a new compositional mentality evolved according to which each formal musical element is seen in relationship to every

would have been familiar with this mode of spatial organization via the paintings of Kandinsky, who claimed to have experienced a revelation in 1911 when hearing a performance of Schoenberg's work in Berlin that included the *Second String Quartet* (op. 10).[2] That quartet, famously, includes a part for soprano in the third and fourth movements. As Dore Ashton has noted,

> Schoenberg found the repetitious phrasing and banally predictable rhyming forms in Viennese music of his youth an offence to his sensibility and intelligence. Since the world no longer appeared governed by the cause and effect symmetries that had so long been taken for granted, it seemed appropriate to release art from the tyranny of symmetrical law and pointless repetition. There were many composers interested at that time in what was loosely called musical prose, just as poets such as Apollinaire were engaged in experiments with 'conversation poems' and free verse.[3]

Ashton states that "[t]he asymmetry of such experiments was spatial. In keeping with post-Euclidean geometry and Einstein's theory of relativity, these experimental spaces had neither up nor down, beginnings nor endings. Once Kandinsky abjured vanishing-point perspective, and once Schoenberg abandoned tonality, there were infinite possibilities,"[4] such that "Schoenberg's spatializing diction, even in his mature years, always harks back to the new conception of musical space of the first decade."[5] *Sprechstimme* was one such spatial innovation. When writing *Pierrot Lunaire,* Schoenberg's "instructions to the singer were that the rhythm and duration of her performance must

---

    other element. There are no schemes, dogmas, recipes, but each moment represents a unique, immutable, necessary possibility that presented itself for realisation at this specific moment" (95).

2 Bojan Bujić, *Arnold Schoenberg* (London: Phaidon, 2011), 82.
3 Dore Ashton, *A Fable of Modern Art* (London: Thames & Hudson, 1980), 108–9.
4 Ibid., 109.
5 Ibid., 110.

be like a conventional sung line but that the intervals and pitch would be — as they are in the natural speaking voice — completely relative. The result is the incomparably moving sense of shifting spaces, infinite gradations in spaces, scarcely graspable transitions that he had begun to envisage as his new structure."[6] The use of *Sprechstimme* and its infinite spaces posed a lifelong problem for Schoenberg, however, in the need to balance "the desire for infinity with some mode of restraining its excesses."[7] This infinity manifests itself in *Moses und Aron* as the unutterable: "[w]hat was to be uttered had to be purged of all extrinsic values, but at the same time had to be the ground on which all motives could honestly subsist. It had to be [...] an 'other' way of expressing the inexpressible," and "[what] he seemed to hear echoing from the abyss was a language that was on the threshold of song."[8] It is precisely on this threshold that Schoenberg situates *Moses und Aron,* a threshold defined by the desert as pure space.

The dynamic of speech and song extends throughout Schoenberg's *oeuvre,* from *Pierrot Lunaire* (1912) to the *Ode for Napoleon* (1942). What we are hearing in these works is Schoenberg's response to a world that is falling apart again and again, and repeatedly reconstituting itself as something quite different. Ezra Pound wrote in 1914 that "[t]here is a sort of poetry where music, sheer melody, seems as if it were just bursting into speech. There is another sort of poetry where painting or sculpture seems as if it were 'just coming over into speech,'"[9] and this sense of liminality and of the uncanny is characteristic of Schoenberg's hybrid art. *Moses und Aron* is about the negotiation of that new space. As Ute Holl writes, "[f]or Schoenberg this space is initially simply the alternative to the prevailing Western tradition of listening and musical meaningfulness. Through musical and media-technical stagings of the voices and

---

6   Ibid., 111.
7   Ibid.
8   Ibid., 114.
9   Ezra Pound, "Vorticism," *Fortnightly Review* 96 n.s. (September 1, 1914), http://fortnightlyreview.co.uk/vorticism/.

instruments, Schoenberg bases the opera's sound space, which emerges with the vocalise, in a hitherto unheard presence of tremendous sonorities. Something is both absolutely there and absolutely alien."[10] *Sprechstimme* embodies this dynamic; it is neither song nor speech but the relationship between them. It is sound with a difference.

The vocal element is fundamental to an understanding of Schoenberg's work. As Adorno put it,

> Schoenberg's instinctive mode of reaction is melodic; everything in him is actually 'sung,' including the instrumental lines. This endows his music with its articulate character, free-moving and yet structural down to the last tone. The primacy of breathing over the beat of abstract time contrasts Schoenberg to Stravinsky and to all those who, having adjusted better to contemporary existence, fancy themselves more modern than Schoenberg. The reified mind is allergic to the elaboration and fulfilment of melody, for which it substitutes the docile repetition of mutilated melodic fragments. The ability to follow the breath of the music unafraid had already distinguished Schoenberg from older, post-Wagnerian composers like Strauss and Wolf, in whom the music seems unable to develop its substance according to its intrinsic impulses and requires literary and programmatic support, even in the songs.[11]

The allusion to program music returns us to Schoenberg's critique of tonality and the concomitant notion of narrative completion. This is precisely what would be lacking in *Moses und Aron*.

---

10 Ute Holl, *The Moses Complex: Freud, Schoenberg, Straub/Huillet,* trans. Michael Turnbull (Zurich & Berlin: Diaphanes, 2017) , 71–72.
11 Theodor W. Adorno, *Prisms,* trans. Samuel and Sherry Weber (Cambridge: MIT Press, 1967), 151.

ten

What Schoenberg was seeking to do in his work was to expand the soundscape beyond traditional notions of what "music" was, an insight that Cage understood intuitively and to which he devoted his career. In arguing that the sonic environment, or soundscape, constituted a form of music, Cage was harkening to the insights of the Futurist artist Luigi Russolo's *L'arte dei rumori*, and if it appears difficult to draw a direct line between Russolo and Schoenberg, one can do so indirectly via Schoenberg's mentor Gustav Mahler.[1] Russolo's *L'arte dei rumori*, the manifesto launched in 1913 and published in the midst of WW1, opens with the observation that, whereas in the past, music was attributed to the gods (and hence its role in religious rites), "today, noise

---

1 Russolo's treatise had been preceded by Ferruccio Busoni's 1907 *Sketch of a New Aesthetic of Music* (translated in 1911 by T. Baker for Schirmer of New York), in which Busoni (who was one of Schoenberg's correspondents) entertains the possibility of electronic music: "I refer to an invention by Dr. Thaddeus Cahill. He has constructed a comprehensive apparatus which makes it possible to transform an electric current into a fixed and mathematically exact number of vibrations. As pitch depends on the number of vibrations, and the apparatus may be 'set' on any number desired, the infinite gradation of the octave may be accomplished by merely moving a lever corresponding to the pointer of a quadrant" (33).

triumphs over and dominates our sensibilities."[2] By "noise," Russolo means an irregular set of vibrations, be it temporally or in terms of intensity; by "sound," he refers to a regular succession of vibrations. Polyphonic music was based on the notion that music developed in time; harmony did not exist in the sense that the various parts of the musical work were subordinate to it. The idea of music, thus, was horizontal, not vertical. The desire for harmony developed gradually, passing from music with little dissonance "to the complicated and persistent dissonances that characterize contemporary music [*alle complicate e persistenti dissonanze che caratterizzano la musica contemporanea*]."[3] This evolution of music, Russolo argues, derives from the increasing proliferation of machines. Its implications are seen, for example, in the increasing size of orchestras, where the goal is to increase the sound produced; the artistic motivation, in other words, is not strictly musical. Given the overriding presence of noise in contemporary culture, music must "conquer the infinite variety of sound-noise [*suono rumore*],"[4] which in a large city includes the rush of gas in metallic tubes, the mumbling of motors, the screeching of brakes, the din of subways, and the sounds associated with modern warfare.[5] In a statement that Cage will echo, Russolo writes that "every manifestation of our life is accompanied by noise."[6] Even language contains noise, represented by consonants; sound is associated with vowels.[7]

The art of noise does not seek to limit itself to imitations of environmental sounds; rather, it is produced by a new set of instruments called *intonarumori* (noisemakers). Russolo notes that the division of the octave into 12 equal tones imposed a considerable limitation on the number of sounds that could be

---

2   Luigi Russolo, *L'arte dei rumori* (Milan: Edizioni Futuriste, 1916), 9, my trans. throughout.
3   Ibid., 10.
4   Ibid., 11.
5   Ibid., 12.
6   Ibid., 14.
7   Ibid., 52.

produced musically, a notion that Cage would fully take up with 4' 33". Russolo remarks that

> the tempered harmonic system can be compared to a system of painting that abolished all the infinite gradations that the seven colors are able to provide[:] [...] one yellow, one green, one red, etc. [...] Temperament with its homophony has in a certain way disconnected the notes, having taken from them the most delicate ties that can unite them and that represent fractions of tones smaller than even semitones.[8]

While this theory of noise may appear to be unacceptable to many, Russolo states, the history of music consistently reminds us that change is the essence of that history:

> Who is surprised any longer by the famous harmonic dissonance of Beethoven's Ninth Symphony? [...] Who thinks to say any longer that the music of Wagner hurts the ears? And the most recent dissonances of Debussy and of Strauss, have they not become logical and normal for our ears?[9]

Russolo goes on to argue that "it wouldn't be possible for music to evolve so decisively towards dissonance if our ears had not been used to the sonic complexities of modern life."[10]

What is crucial to note in Russolo's tract is that dissonance is accompanied by an extension of the soundscape, expanding, thus, the musical domain. Schoenberg confronted this extension via the influence of Gustav Mahler, who was composing music in Vienna at a time when it had the reputation of "the world's leading center for Jewish liturgical music."[11] Uri Caine's

---

8   Ibid., 60.
9   Ibid., 89.
10 Ibid., 90.
11 Alexander L. Ringer, *Arnold Schoenberg: The Composer as Jew* (Oxford: Clarendon Press, 1990), 8.

album *Urlicht/Primal Light*,[12] brings out the connections brilliantly. As Caine has stated in an interview,

> I had read a story about Mahler, in the Henry-Louis de la Grange biography, about how he was conducting in Prague and met a great singer at the opera. Turned out the guy was a cantor [musical leader of a synagogue] and not a professional singer. So they spent an afternoon together, where, in a way, the cantor was trying to persuade Mahler to return to Judaism, because Mahler had had to convert [from Judaism to Catholicism at age 37, to secure a court appointment], and Mahler was sort of defending himself. And when he listened to the cantor's music, he was crying, he was moved. … The [melody of] the opening of 'The Farewell,' which Mahler wrote at the end of his life as one of the pieces in *The Song of the Earth* (*Das Lied von der Erde*) I had heard at a Jewish funeral, in the *Prayer for the Dead*. So [in 'Mahler: Reimagined'] we're having a cantor, Don Gurney, from L.A. He sings that prayer, and we improvise around it, and then we play Mahler.[13]

Franz Winter states in the liner notes to the CD that,

> [o]n the cusp of a new era, [Mahler's] music is the Janus-like embodiment of the crisis in sound. He is collector, preserver and destroyer. In the shadow of Wagner, in the fading aura of Bruckner, it is he who once more strives to restore expressive grandeur to music. And he interweaves and instills it with all imaginable trivial sounds of his time: with marches, dance

---

12 Gustav Mahler/Uri Caine, *Urlicht/Primal Light,* Winter & Winter, 910 004-2, 1997, compact disc.
13 Jeff Kaliss, "Praising Uri Caine," *San Francisco Classical Voice,* June 4, 2014, https://www.sfcv.org/events-calendar/artist-spotlight/praising-uri-caine; square brackets are in the original. Caine says in the same interview that he is a great fan of Glenn Gould.

music, folk music, with cowbells and sleigh bells, with rattles and mallets.[14]

Schoenberg did something similar with the "klezmer-ish touches" in his orchestration of Brahms's *G Minor Quartet*,[15] but, more significantly, he wanted to do this from within the musical system, his profound insight being that such difference was always already an intrinsic part of the musical environment.

---

14 Franz Winter, "Gustave Mahler (1860–1911)," liner notes, Gustav Mahler/ Uri Caine, *Urlicht/Primal Light*.
15 James R. Oestreich, "Works with Hélène Grimaud, Daniel Barenboim and Others," *New York Times,* May 6, 2016, https://www.nytimes.com/2016/05/07/arts/music/review-works-by-helene-grimaud-daniel-barenboim-and-others.html.

eleven

One of the most notorious "environmental" sounds in Gould's recordings is his humming and singing, and it has occasioned considerable commentary by those who have written about him, a number of them ascribing this performance trait to Gould's supposed autism. What particularly concerned Gould's critics is that the singing and humming that accompanied his performances undermined their concept of a perfectionist Gould who employed technology to achieve the perfect performance.[1] The humming on the recordings, however, can be understood as willfully moving in the opposite direction, declaring that the performance is contingent, embodied, and, above all, mediated.[2] Roland Barthes has written compellingly of this phenomenon:

> What does the body *do* when it enunciates (musically)? [...] [M]y body strikes, my body collects itself, it explodes, it divides, it pricks, or on the contrary and without warning,

---

[1] Michael Sanden comments that, for Gould, "audio recording would seem to be the perfect medium through which he could exercise his mind-centered approach to performance." See *Liveness in Modern Music* (New York: Routledge, 2012), 51.

[2] To quote Sanden again, there is a "very real potential for sound technology to further increase a listener's engagement with corporeality in mediatized music" (ibid., 52).

> [...] it stretches out, it weaves. [...] And sometimes — why not — it even speaks, it declaims, it doubles its voice: *it speaks but says nothing*: for as soon as it is musical, speech — or its instrumental substitute — is no longer linguistic but corporeal; what it says is always and only this: *my body puts itself in a state of speech: quasi parlando.*[3]

In vocal music, *parlando* (literally, "speaking") is a "directive for the tone of the voice to approximate to speech," and in instrumental music "it calls for an expressive freedom greater than is implied by *cantabile*."[4] These references to speaking imply that music is mediated (including, as in Barthes's formulation, by the body of the performer), that it is not a "pure" mode of expression, that it is "in the world," and one of the most astounding aspects of Schoenberg's twelve tone compositions is that they are able to assert this belongingness through an apparently abstract musical idiom. Gould's sound documentaries declare their belongingness from the other direction: they translate speech into various musical idioms, taking the human voice and orchestrating it acoustically as an "oral tone poem" or "verbal quintet."[5] Gould stated that his documentaries derived from the realization that "much of the new music has a lot to do with the spoken word, with the rhythms and patterns, the rise and fall and inclination, the ordering of phrase and regulation of cadence in human speech. [...] I think our whole notion of what music is has forever merged with all the sounds that are around us, everything that the environment makes available."[6] In his piano performances, Gould's humming has a similar effect; as Edward

---

[3] Roland Barthes, "Rasch," in *The Responsibility of Forms: Critical Essays on Music, Art and Representation,* trans. Richard Howard (New York: Hill and Wang, 1985), 305–6, emphasis in original.

[4] "Parlando," in *Concise Oxford Dictionary of Music,* eds. Michael Kennedy and Joyce Bourne Kennedy (Oxford: Oxford University Press, 2007), 691.

[5] See Richard Cavell, *McLuhan in Space: A Cultural Geography* (Toronto: University of Toronto Press, 2002), 164.

[6] Quoted by Geoffrey Payzant, *Glenn Gould: Music and Mind* (Toronto: Van Nostrand Reinhold, 1978), 130, from Gould's 1970 CBC telecast "The Well-Tempered Listener."

Said puts it, "humming over and above the piano's sound" has the effect of "extend[ing] the piano's reach into verbal language."[7]

With these paradoxical relationships of music and language, singing and speaking, we begin to approach the complexities of *Moses und Aron*. The overriding antinomy of the opera, based on a single tone row,[8] is well-known: Moses the prophet can only communicate via *Sprechstimme*; Aron can sing but is denied Moses' knowledge — not "vision," because what Moses knows does not derive from the visual domain. His knowledge is given to him by the Voice of God, which first sings, acousmatically, before the curtain rises, and then speaks from the burning bush, a visual image which negates itself — it is there and not there. In fact, Schoenberg allowed for the possibility that these voices be transmitted electronically from offstage.[9] The dynamics of the opera's plot can be understood in terms of Moses' need to communicate his prophecy and the impossibility of doing so, since God is "infinite, inconceivable."[10] Schoenberg once said to Bertolt Brecht (his neighbor in Los Angeles) that "music lacks purely musical conceptual material,"[11] which restates, in formal terms, the dilemma posed by the opera. The music of the opera is a "saying" that is a "not saying," which encapsulates the prob-

---

[7] Edward Said, "The Music Itself: Glenn Gould's Contrapuntal Vision," in *Glenn Gould: Variations* (Toronto: Doubleday, 1983), 50.

[8] As Arnfinn Bø-Rygg, among others, has noted. See "The Finished Fragment: On Arnold Schoenberg's *Moses und Aron*," in *Transcendence and Sensoriness: Perceptions, Revelation, and the Arts,* eds. Svein Aage Christofferson et al. (Leiden: Brill 2015), 257.

[9] As Schoenberg's son-in-law Luigi Nono pointed out, "[t]he idea of spacing out the music of the Burning Bush with electronic means goes back, of course, to Schoenberg's indication that the six speaking voices representing the 'voice from the Burning Bush' could be separated from each other offstage 'using telephones which will lead through loudspeakers into the hall where the voices will then coalesce'" (internal quotation from Schoenberg's staging notes). See Carola Nielinger-Vakil, *Luigi Nono: A Composer in Context* (Cambridge: Cambridge University Press, 2015), 91.

[10] Karl H. Wörner, *Schoenberg's "Moses and Aaron,"* trans. Paul Hamburger (London: Faber and Faber, 1963), 112.

[11] Hanns Eisler, *Brecht, Music and Culture: Hanns Eisler in Conversation with Hans Bunge* (London: Bloomsbury, 2014), 51.

lematic of the opera as enacted through *Sprechstimme*, a singing that is not singing, neither speech nor song. The paradox of the opera functions in a way that is similar to the inexpressibility *topos* in literature. A major example of the *topos* occurs at the end of Dante's *Commedia* (another *Exodus* story), where the poet, granted a vision of God, must confess himself unable to express this vision: "All'alta fantasia qui mancò possa."[12] Paradoxically, however, this *does* succeed in conveying the ineffability of the vision. Dante is able to speak of his vision by not speaking of it. We are likewise confronted by uncanny doublings and an expression of lack in the last lines of the (completed) opera: "O word, thou word, that I lack." It is significant that the "word" that Moses "lacks" occurs twice, and that his speech is accompanied by violins — the instrument considered to be closest to the human voice. This "lack" is congruent with the Lacanian *manque*, and once again it is accompanied by a doubling, by an excess of signification. The opera as a whole is mapped onto this doubling; as Michael Cherlin describes it, in addition to the doubling of Moses and Aron, and the movement of the folk between collectivity and individuation, there are the two aspects of the Divine Voice, "both polyphonic in nature: there is a disembodied aspect, composed of six solo voices, each of which is doubled by an instrument, and there is a second aspect, visually [*sic*] manifest through the burning bush, musically composed of a speaking choir."[13] As Cherlin further notes, "the two brothers each articulate one aspect of the Divine Voice, speaking or singing."[14] In other words, they together articulate the notion of the Divine Voice as mediate, as a "'carrying across' in the literal meaning of the Latin word *translatio*; a process that produces

---

12 Dante Alighieri, "Paradiso" 33.142, in *La divina commedia*, ed. Giorgio Petrocchi (Turin: Einaudi, 1975), 412: "my powers of imagination here failed me," my trans.

13 Michael Cherlin, "Schoenberg's Music for the Theater," in *The Great Tradition and its Legacy: The Evolution of Dramatic and Musical Theater in Austria and Central Europe*, eds. Michael Cherlin et al. (New York: Berghahn, 2004), 254.

14 Ibid., 255.

values of which the spoken word itself is not capable," as Karl Wörner put it.[15] Translation, as McLuhan noted, is the fundamental process of all media,[16] and in this context it is significant that the opening sounds of the opera emerge from behind the stage curtain; the opera becomes about the translation of these opening sounds into the dramatic (ontological, epistemological) action. The curtain itself recalls the drapery employed by Pythagoras during his lectures, which he stood behind in order "to lend [his voice] a somewhat divine authority,"[17] the allusion bringing together the notion of divinity and the concept of music as represented by the Pythagoras whose musical scale had twelve pitches that were mathematically related (and in whose orbit R. Murray Schafer placed Schoenberg). As acousmatic sound (a sound whose origin is obscure), the opening moments of the opera align with recorded music as well, and recall electro-acoustic composer Pierre Schaeffer's comment that "the tape recorder has the virtue of Pythagoras' curtain,"[18] because the source of the originating sound is not present. As Kittler suggested, with electronic media we reinvent the voice of the gods, a voice beyond the human.[19] By placing this divine expression of pure sound at the *beginning* of his opera, Schoenberg reverses the teleological resolution of Wagner's *Liebestod*; in *Moses und Aron,* the thematic "resolution" is at the beginning: pure sound,

---

15 Wörner, *Schoenberg's "Moses and Aaron,"* 85.
16 As Marshall McLuhan states, "[a]ll media are active metaphors in their power to translate experience into new forms." See *Understanding Media: The Extensions of Man* (New York: McGraw-Hill, 1964), 57.
17 Dominic Pettman, *Sonic Intimacy: Voice, Species, Technics* (Stanford: Stanford University Press, 2017), 28. Brian Kane's historical analysis in *Sound Unseen: Acousmatic Sound in Theory and Practice* (Oxford: Oxford University Press, 2016) disputes the existence of a veil, but electro-acoustic composer Pierre Schaeffer suggests that the value of the concept is in the metaphor, especially as it applies to the electronic reproduction of sound.
18 Quoted by Pettman, *Sonic Intimacy,* 28, from Pierre Schaeffer's essay on "Acousmatics" in *Audio Culture: Readings in Modern Music* (New York: Continuum, 2004), 76–81.
19 Friedrich Kittler, "The God of the Ears," in *The Truth of the Technological World,* ed. Hans Ulrich Gumbrecht (Stanford: Stanford University Press, 2013), 45–56.

sound not yet burdened with meaning. The opera is not moving toward resolution; it is moving away from it in its insistence on sound as mediation, as process.

Schoenberg sets *Moses und Aron* in this translational context, as Wörner has suggested. Much of the dialogue between Moses and Aron constitutes a dispute about how to translate the Divine Word into a human context, and *Sprechstimme* is itself a mode of translation, placing words in constant movement, from speaking to singing, from singing to speaking. This dynamic characterizes the opera as a whole. As Cherlin points out, the opera begins not with a word, however, but with a sound, "O," sung by the six solo voices. "O" is the domain *par excellence* of orality. In Bruce R. Smith's characterization, "O" is "semantically empty," which is to say that its meaning cannot be assigned with any specificity by virtue of the fact that it says everything: it is the verbal modality of plenitude. When Othello, learning that Iago has duped him into believing that Desdemona was unfaithful to him, says "Oh, oh, oh,"[20] he is making sounds that attempt to communicate what words cannot. As Smith puts it, "O" is a "an *environmental* gesture"; "the environment certainly includes plants and animals, but it also includes air, ink, fiber-optic cable — and other people."[21] Jan Assmann has argued in *Moses the Egyptian* that whereas "[i]n the polytheistic world of ancient Egypt, religion had been a medium of translation and communication [...] [whereby] the Greek sun-god Apollo corresponded to the Egyptian sun-god Re[,] Dionysus was another name for Bacchus[,] and Zeus was translatable as Jupiter," this changed "in the new world of monotheism, [when] religion became a barrier to communication: the names for God became not only untranslatable, but also unpronounce-

---

20 William Shakespeare, "Othello, the Moore of Venice," in *The Complete Works of William Shakespeare 3: Tragedies* (London: Nonesuch Press, 1953), act 5, scene 2.
21 Bruce R. Smith, *The Acoustic World of Early Modern England: Attending to the O-Factor* (Chicago: University of Chicago Press, 1999), 14.

able and unrepresentable."[22] But there is another act of translation at work here, that between orality and literacy, between the divine voice and the graven tablets. Orality is the law (*nomos*) that existed before the law in the same way that the divine voice precedes the beginning of the opera: the law was sung before it was spoken, and spoken before it was written. As Alex Rehding notes, the opening moments of the opera defy the opera's tone row;[23] they operate according to another law of creation that has its parallel in the Oral Torah that reigned until the destruction of the Temple in 70 CE, when the Jews became The People of the Book. As with *Sprechstimme,* it is the interplay of the oral and the written, the sung and the spoken, that defines the dynamics of the opera.

Cherlin writes that it is only with words that Moses can respond to the divine "O": "[h]is list of divine attributes moves through a progression of vowels — *E*izinger, *e*wiger, *a*llgegenwärtige, *u*nsichtbarer und *u*nvorstellbarer G*o*tt — that approach but never reach the original 'O,'"[24] and that are engulfed by hard consonantal sounds. From the beginning, then, Schoenberg directs our attention to the tensions between the vocalic and the consonantal that underlie the history of alphabetic culture as well as the music libel of the Jews. To the vocalic utterance of the Divine Voice, Moses can reply only with consonant-laden *Sprechstimme* (as Holl notes above). This identifies the opening scene as that of a world fallen from singing into speaking, from orality into literacy.[25] As Kittler reminds us, "the gods came because they were rhythmically and melodically invoked."[26] Mo-

---

22 As summarized by Eliza Slavet, "A Matter of Distinction: On Recent Work by Jan Assmann," *AJS Review* 34, no. 2 (2010): 387.
23 Alex Rehding, "Moses's Beginning," *Opera Quarterly* 2, no. 4 (2007): 395–417.
24 Cherlin, "Schoenberg's Music for the Theater," 256; first line of libretto. Cherlin reiterates this point in *Schoenberg's Musical Imagination* (Cambridge: Cambridge University Press, 2007), 283.
25 These tensions are brilliantly explored by Willy Decker in his 2009 staging of the opera for the Ruhrtriennale.
26 Friedrich Kittler, "Pathos and Ethos: An Aristotelian Observation," in *The Truth of the Technological World,* 304–5.

ses, however, is unable to sing. When, after forty days, Moses descends from the mountain, he condemns the golden calf as an attempt to visualize the unvisualizable, and Aron replies that the tablets Moses is bearing are likewise graven images. To quote Kittler again: "[n]o image floating before our eyes compares in its pathos to what speaks in the voice [*aus der Stimme*]."[27] Moses' destruction of the tablets has the effect of re-asserting the primacy of orality.

Beatrice Hanssen addresses the paradoxes of the opera in her comment on Adorno's famous revision of his stricture against poetry after the Holocaust: "Recognizing that the suffering should not be forgotten, Adorno now revises his insight: the suffering at once demands art's continuation and simultaneously prohibits art's production. Experimental artworks, which explicitly reflect on the incommensurability of their form, might be able to do justice to this double task. Less likely to succeed, by contrast, are artworks that labor under the illusion of 'immediacy' as they directly lend voice to the suffering."[28] How to express "art's continuation" and it prohibition? Moses is caught between these antinomies, caught between media, caught between an unseen voice and a graven text. As Holl puts it, "Moses is a media complex."[29] *Sprechstimme* in this context must be counted a divine gift: its dissonance constitutes at once Schoenberg's response to the music libel against the Jews and the hybrid medium which allows him to express his knowledge while respecting the "inconceivable."[30]

---

27 Ibid., 305.
28 Beatrice Hanssen, "Dissonance and Aesthetic Totality: Adorno Reads Schönberg," in *Sound Figures of Modernity: German Music and Philosophy*, eds. Jost Hermand and Gerhard Richter (Madison: University of Wisconsin Press, 2006), 196–97.
29 Ute Holl, *The Moses Complex: Freud, Schoenberg, Straub/Huillet,* trans. Michael Turnbull (Zurich & Berlin: Diaphanes, 2017), 301.
30 Julian Johnson comments that "music is not philosophy. […] [U]nlike philosophy, music has necessarily to mediate between its particular materials (the sensuous physicality of timbre, rhythm, intensity) and their abstract, intellectual ordering (as phrase, section, form). Whereas philosophy is thought in the abstract medium of language, music is

What remains at the end (of Act Two) of the opera is music, sound,[31] which *can* speak the unspeakable — *quasi parlando* — precisely by not speaking. HaCohen notes that in *Moses und Aron,* the "unsynchronized, disjointed atonal soundscape uttered by many voices contrasts, in the opera, with the rhythmized, tonalized world of the golden calf rites."[32] HaCohen asks about these tensions between tonality and atonality: "[a]re those who [...] are enveloped by it — the protagonists in their fictive world — aware, however slightly, of the nature of the medium in which they express themselves? Or is the medium a message solely addressed to those outside the protagonists' world, that is, to attentive listeners [...]?"[33] In an oral culture, ontological questions such as these ultimately defer to the medium through which being is experienced; in a literate culture, as she suggests, one must listen carefully. Ultimately, the medium of the opera is its message — not the position put forward by Moses (who by the end of the opera is no further along than at the beginning) and certainly not the position put forward by Aron. It is the medium of sound that does what neither Moses nor Aron can do, which is to express the inexpressible. "Unconsciously," sings Aron, "we have done thy will."[34] What repeatedly asserts itself in the opera is the dissonance between the positions of the brothers, and of their musical modalities. In his discussion of disso-

---

thought through the concrete medium of its sonic materials." See "Schoenberg, Modernism and Metaphysics," in *The Cambridge Companion to Schoenberg,* eds. Jennifer Shaw and Joseph Auner (Cambridge: Cambridge University Press, 2010), 118.

31 As Richard Kurth writes, "[t]he music's fabric of sound, more than the events portrayed or the ideas articulated by the words, conveys the experience and import of [the opera's] epistemological limits." See "Immanence and Transcendence in *Moses und Aron,*" in *The Cambridge Companion to Schoenberg,* 177.

32 Ruth HaCohen, *The Music Libel against the Jews* (New Haven: Yale University Press, 2011), 311.

33 Ibid., 324.

34 This is HaCohen's paraphrase (ibid., 325) of "Unbewußt wird getan, wie du willst," which Paul Hamburger translates in the libretto as "Unbeknown, what you want will be done," in Karl H. Wörner, *Schoenberg's "Moses and Aaron,"* trans. Paul Hamburger (London: Faber and Faber, 1963), 189.

nance in the *Theory of Harmony,* Schoenberg writes that "[t]wo impulses struggle with each other within man: the demand for repetition of pleasant stimuli, and the opposing desire for variety, for change, for a new stimulus."[35] These opposing impulses are reconciled through the creation of a system, which allows for breaches on the understanding that they will ultimately be resolved. The great danger, argues Schoenberg, is that the system will be treated as natural. "But that the system is false, or at least inadequate, because it cannot accommodate phenomena that do exist, or labels them trash, exceptions, accidental harmonic structures, piles of rejects — that ha[s] to be said."[36] Thus, writes, Schoenberg, "[t]here are [...] no non-harmonic tones, no tones foreign to harmony, but merely tones foreign to the harmonic system."[37]

This idea emerges powerfully in Schoenberg's correspondence with Wassily Kandinsky. Writing after they had both published major works — Schoenberg the *Theory of Harmony* (1911) and Kandinsky *On the Spiritual in Art* (1910) — and after Kandinsky had heard the *Second String Quartet* (op. 10), we find Kandinsky writing about visual art in terms associated with Schoenberg's Theory of Harmony[38] in an extraordinary letter (22 August 1912) that merits quoting *in extenso*:

> The fact is that the greatest necessity for musicians today is the overthrow of the 'eternal laws of harmony,' which for painters is only a matter of secondary importance. [...] [W]hen one departs from the root [of all forms of expres-

---

35 Arnold Schoenberg, *Theory of Harmony,* trans. Roy Carter (Berkeley: University of California Press, 1978), 48.
36 Ibid., 321.
37 Ibid.
38 Portions of the *Theory of Harmony* had been published in a journal in the fall of 1910, and there was a quotation from the *Theory* on the poster for the 1911 concert of Schoenberg's music that Kandinsky had heard. This occasioned the first letter Kandinsky sent to Schoenberg in January of 1911. See Jelena Hahl-Koch, ed., *Arnold Schoenberg / Wassily Kandinsky: Letters, Pictures and Documents,* trans. John C. Crawford (London: Faber, 1984), 21.

sion], every possibility of combination becomes an 'or the opposite.' But sometimes one is forced to illumine only *one* side glaringly and obtrusively. [...] *Unfortunately,* only a few can grasp this 'or the opposite,' and this is the reason the Ten Commandments were also given only one-sidedly and 'positively.' [...] I will show, however, that construction is also to be attained by the 'principle' of dissonance. [...] This is what people call 'anarchy,' by which they understand a kind of lawlessness (since they can see only *one* side of the Ten Commandments) and by which they must come to understand order (in art, construction), but one which has its roots in another sphere.³⁹

The references to the Ten Commandments return us to *Moses und Aron* and suggest that the commandments be understood in an artistic or mediatic sense. If we recall Adorno's comment that "*Moses und Aron* is *musica ficta,*" and that *musica ficta* was considered to be a way of avoiding the "devil in music," then this passage can be understood as mapping the central drama of *Moses und Aron*⁴⁰ and of the musical career of Arnold Schoen-

---

39 Ibid., 57.
40 Adorno comments that "[t]he opera *Moses und Aron* is *musica ficta,*" and, as Beatrice Hanssen reminds us, "since medieval times, [...] *musica ficta* — or unacceptable chromatic modulations — [was linked] to the mythical figure of the devil. Driven by superstition, the church placed a ban on so-called dissonant, devilish chords, or tritones, the *diabolus in musica* (the devil in music)." See Theodor W. Adorno, "Sacred Fragment," in *Quasi una fantasia,* trans. Rodney Livingstone (London: Verso, 1992), 225–48, and Beatrice Hanssen, "Dissonance and Aesthetic Totality:Adorno Reads Schönberg," in *Sound Figures of Modernity: German Music and Philosophy,* eds. Jost Hermand and Gerhard Richter (Madison: University of Wisconsin Press, 2006), 189. In musicological terms, from the 9th or 10th century through the Renaissance, "the tritone, nicknamed the '*diabolus in musica,*' was regarded as an unstable interval and rejected as a consonance by most theorists." See "Tritone," *The New Grove Dictionary of Music and Musicians,* ed. Stanley Sadie, 2nd edn. (London: Macmillan, 2001), 25: 747–49. The term *musica ficta* was used "to designate 'feigned' extensions of the hexachord system contained in the so-called Guidonian hand. [...] In modern usage, the term *musica ficta* is often loosely applied to all unnotated inflections inferred from the context" (ibid., 17: 441).

berg. What Gould understood about that drama was its claim that the media of contemporary art were shifting from visual to acoustic space.

Sir Ernest Macmillan notes that "*musica ficta* — literally 'feigned music' [...] signifies the flattening of the B or the sharpening of the F," and that these changes were made in order to avoid the awkward interval of the tritone or augmented fourth, which medieval theorists called 'the devil in music.'" See *Macmillan on Music: Essays by Sir Ernest Macmillan* (Toronto: Dundurn Press, 1997), 165. *Sprechstimme,* through its vocal "in betweenness," strikes me as the locus *par excellence* of *musica ficta,* and in this understanding Adorno's application of the term to *Moses und Aron* gains additional resonance.

twelve

The move toward configuring an acoustic space of performance congruent with that of composed theater and sound installations was anticipated by Gould in his acoustic orchestrations of the 1970s.[1] These "orchestrations" are not musical but mediatic.[2] As McLuhan wrote in 1951,

> [o]rchestration permits discontinuity and endless variety. [...] It is a conception inherent not only in symbolist art but in quantum and relativity physics. Unlike Newtonian physics, it can entertain a harmony that is not unilateral, monistic, or tyrannical. It is neither progressive nor reactionary but

---

[1] In this section I am drawing on my discussion of Gould in Richard Cavell, *McLuhan in Space: A Cultural Geography* (Toronto: University of Toronto Press, 2002), 156–69.

[2] See, for example, Blair Sanderson's review of the recording of Gould's acoustic orchestrations. While acknowledging that Gould was "trying out new ways to capture spatial relations in sound," Sanderson argues that "the only 'orchestration' involved is the manipulation of piano sonorities, dynamics, and the directions from which the music was recorded; there is no orchestra involved." Blair Sanderson, review of "Glenn Gould, *The Acoustic Orchestrations — Works by Scriabin and Sibelius*," *AllMusic*, https://www.allmusic.com/album/glenn-gould-the-acoustic-orchestrations-works-by-scriabin-and-sibelius-mw0002428189.

embraces all previous actualizations [...] while welcoming the new in a simultaneous present.[3]

Unlike visual space, whose parameters are given, acoustic space is created by sound; it is this distinction that marks Gould's retirement from the concert hall and his turn to recording, a move that channeled the mediatic shift from the visual space produced by print culture to the acoustic space of electronic media. This shift is apparent in the use of headphones, which lack a visual orientation, as opposed to the figure/ground, or piano/forte space of the concert hall. The deeply involving nature of electronic media has the effect of making the consumer of music into a producer (which is brought out in the remastered recordings issued by Sony under the title *Glenn Gould: Acoustic Orchestrations,* where the disc allows the listener to program the music[4]), breaking down, thus, the hierarchy of art and non-art in the process of making / poeisis through which art becomes environmental.

Gould's acoustic orchestration of the fifth Scriabin sonata is remarkable in this context. Employing the acoustic orchestration process, Gould arranged ranks of microphones around the piano in order to produce a cubistic or mosaic sonic orientation that

---

3   Marshall McLuhan, *The Mechanical Bride: Folklore of Industrial Man* (New York: Vanguard Press, 1951), 34.
4   Glenn Gould, *The Acoustic Orchestrations: Works by Scriabin and Sibelius,* recorded July 16–17, 1970, Sony Classical 887254065722, 2012, compact disc. From the album cover: "'I have a feeling that the end result of all our labors in the recording studio is not going to be some kind of autocratic finished product,' said Glenn Gould; 'we're going to make kits, and I think we're going to send out these kits to listeners. [...] *Be in fact your own editor; be, in a sense, your own performer.*' [...] For the first time ever, these mixes from the 1970s have all been put together as a sensational listening experience (Disc 1) with a Gouldian 'kit' (Disc 2): the edited, stereo tracks containing the four microphone perspectives from the 1970 Scriabin recording sessions. These tracks can be imported into a computer or mobile device, and, in conjunction with a variety of available multitrack applications, used for creating your own mix." I am grateful to Professor Raviv Ganchrow (Institute of Sonology) for his illuminating discussions with me of these recordings on my visit to The Hague in 2017.

was analogous to McLuhan's concept of acoustic space. Gould elaborated this notion in his performance of some Scriabin preludes for a 1974 CBC television production titled "The Age of Ecstasy (1900–1910)," in which his performance was accompanied by swirling colors which sought to convey Scriabin's idea that musical notes had chromatic analogues. The television broadcast of a Webern performance was accompanied by "rapidly changing patterns of colored dots, squares, diamonds, triangles, diamonds, simple shapes that kept expanding and contracting, multiplying and dividing, changing into each other."[5] In an unpublished article on Gould written circa 1966,[6] McLuhan writes of the dilemma facing contemporary piano performers who are confronted by the "continuous visual space" of the concert hall and an audience whose experience of music was increasingly that of the "tactile proximity" afforded by the recording. Gould sought to address this dilemma through his acoustic orchestrations, which would have the additional advantage of engaging the listener analytically. In his copy of Adorno's *Prisms,* Gould underlined in ink the passage in which Adorno comments that the difficulty of Schoenberg's music "requires the listener spontaneously to compose its inner movement and demands of him not mere contemplation but praxis."[7] Technology, in this context, was not a way of removing the performer from the world but engaging the performer with listeners. As Gould stated in an interview, his eccentricities of performance — most notably the humming — should be considered Brechtian,[8] which is another way of saying that the interface of the oral (phono) and the literate (graph) produced by the recording had become environmental in the acoustic space of secondary orality.

---

5 Otto Friedrich, *Glenn Gould: A Life and Variations* (Toronto: Lester and Orpen Dennys, 1989), 218.
6 McLuhan fonds, National Archives of Canada, vol. 99, file 24.
7 Theodor W. Adorno, *Prisms,* trans. Samuel and Sherry Weber (Cambridge: MIT Press, 1967), 149–50.
8 Jonathan Cott, *Conversations with Glenn Gould* (Boston: Little Brown, 1984), 54.

Sound environments (or installations) have increasingly become a defining aspect of the media of contemporary art. Musicologist Helga de la Motte-Haber writes that, with the "new availability of sound material[,] an art form congealed that overstepped traditional boundaries. [...] Visual artists no longer had a monopoly on structuring space. [...] New forms of art arose that lay claim to simultaneous existence in space and time."[9] De la Motte-Haber goes on to remark that, "[p]erhaps owing to its liminal position between more established disciplines, however, sound installation art remains under-recognized within historical accounts of twentieth-century art and music."[10] To this observation, Gascia Ouzounian adds that

> [s]ound installation art has undoubtedly recovered and reoriented the sonic–spatial imagination. [...] When space is understood not in abstract or absolute terms, but as socially and politically constituted, a spatial sound practice can emerge not only as a poetics, but as a politics, not only as an aesthetics, but as an ethics.[11]

Among such works is Stephen Prina's *The Structural Analysis and Reconstruction of MS7098 as Determined by the Differences Between the Measurements of Duration and Displacement* (1990), an artwork that interrogates the solo piano music of Arnold Schoenberg as recorded by Glenn Gould. As Dominic Eichler describes it, the work consists of "a small maplewood table, a couple of chairs, a promotional poster (marketing Gould as a sexy, brooding genius), and headphones attached to a record

---

9 Helga de la Motte-Haber, "Space–Environment–Shared World: Robin Minard's Sound Installations," in *Robin Minard: Silent Music/Between Sound Art and Acoustic Design*, ed. B. Schulz (Heidelberg : Kehrer, 1999), 35.
10 Ibid., 36.
11 Gascia Ouzounian, "Sound Installation Art," in *Music, Sound and Space: Transformations of Public and Private Experience* (Cambridge: Cambridge University Press, 2013), 73.

player."[12] The heart of the exhibition, however was a re-recording made by Prina of Gould's album performing Schoenberg's piano compositions. Eichler notes that "Prina reworked and then re-pressed the LP, taking his compositional cue from the space between the tracks of the original, [...] repositioning 21 seconds of silence in Gould's recording."[13] At the same time that he was producing this work, Prina was planning one which was meant to address Schoenberg's *Six Little Piano Pieces* (op. 19), titled *To the People of Frankfurt am Main: Former Site of Reconstructed Schoenberg Study, Arnold Schoenberg Institute, Room 201, University of Southern California, Los Angeles, Reconstructed at Arnold Schönberg Center, Vienna, 2000*. According to Eichler,

> Schönberg [sic] wanted to make time and space collapse in his music, a typically hardcore modernist aim which Prina apparently thought the composer hadn't entirely achieved. The planned work involved playing all six pieces simultaneously on 1081 loud-speakers (one for each note in the Opus), arranged in concentric circles, in an attempt to create an abstract and singular cacophony, i.e. to finally get something close to what Arnold always wanted.[14]

While dissonance is not cacaphony, the emphasis on sound in Prina's work is a significant intervention in terms of Schoenberg's overall aesthetic. Eichler notes that what these works have in common is

> the meticulous superimpositions of art and culture from various historical periods, media and disciplines. Regardless of each particular work's guise and form (including paintings, installations, photography, graphic works, films, and performances), they all seem to concern the articulation of

---

12 Dominic Eichler, "Point Counter Point," *Frieze*, May 5, 2009, https://frieze.com/article/point-counter-point.
13 Ibid.
14 Ibid.

the resulting resonances and multiple overtones of difference in a contextual flux.[15]

This is to say that what Prina works with — his medium — is art as a total environment, rather than as a particular form of art. That environment includes the work of Jean-Marie Straub and Danièle Huillet, who produced the legendary film of *Moses und Aron* that Ute Holl analyses in *The Moses Complex*; the writings of Roland Barthes and Theodor W. Adorno; conceptualist work by artists such as Lawrence Weiner and Ed Ruscha; and works by composers from Anton von Webern to Steely Dan. This *mélange* is most often associated with postmodernism, and is related to the breaking down of artistic hierarchies and defined historical eras that Schoenberg encountered when he moved to Hollywood, whose architecture alone, apart from the historical mashup produced by the movie industry, gave the incontrovertible death blow to Adorno's notion of artistic progress. Art had shifted from a linear notion of progress, whereby one artistic moment succeeds another, to a spatial notion whereby all artistic moments exist simultaneously. In the domain of musical composition, this idea of artistic co-existence was facilitated through the vast power of retrieval inherent in the medium of recording.

Prina attributes his artistic awakening to the influence of John Cage[16] and a reading of Adorno's *In Search of Wagner*:

> Adorno's dismantling of the notion of the *Gesamtkunstwerk* helped me see that my goal might not be to synthesize the arts but to make discrete forays into multiple disciplines, confident that those pursuits would share underlying structural connections. By the mid-'80s, I understood that my interests were taxonomic, addressed to general principles

---

15 Ibid.
16 Allie Biswas, "Stephen Prina," *Studio International,* May 17, 2016, http://www.studiointernational.com/index.php/stephen-prina-interview-galesburg-illinois.

and particular histories across a range of esthetic practices. Pursuing that diversity has been an important aspect of my career.[17]

The principle here is not one of integration but of juxtaposition, of the relationality of the parts rather than the monolithic presence of the whole. Nor does the artwork have a single context. As pointed out by the writer and theorist Nuit Banai,

> Prina reveals the basic condition of exile that was always constitutive of the modernist art object and that continues to stimulate contemporary art production. Because an art work does not exist without social visibility, it is fated to perpetually wander the globe in search of its next public venue. Like migratory communities such as the circus or the solitary transience of the travelling salesman, the work is expected to simultaneously entertain, edify, and market itself in order to survive.[18]

The signal moment of that sense of exile occurred in Weimar on the Pacific. Here was the definitive break with European cultural hegemony via a renunciation of the *translatio studii,* the idea that there was a linear transfer of culture that followed the course of empire. With the powerful ability of electronic media to retrieve the past, modernism, as McLuhan noted, had gone into reverse.[19] Mann's rewriting of the Faust myth would issue not from Vienna or Berlin but from Pacific Palisades. Given Schoenberg's break with musical history — not in the service

---

17 From an interview with Steel Stillman, "In The Studio: Stephen Prina," *Art in America,* April 26, 2013, http://www.artinamericamagazine.com/news-features/magazines/in-the-studio-stephen-prina.

18 Nuit Banai, quoted by Pedro de Llano, "Displacement and Translation in the Work of Stephen Prina," *Afterall,* September 7, 2009, https://afterall.org/online/displacement.and.translation.in.the.work.of.stephen.prina.

19 See the chapter "Reversal of the Overheated Medium," in Marshall McLuhan, *Understanding Media: The Extensions of Man* (New York: McGraw-Hill, 1964), 33–40.

of progress, but in the service of a return to musical foundations — it is not surprising that we find him at the center of Mann's story, the unnamed other of a cultural tradition that was now folding back on itself through a series of negative involutions, Schoenberg's journey ending where Gould's began, in the west beyond the (Hegelian/Spenglerian) West.

Prina has stated in an interview that his artwork is informed by "the well known French cultural theorist Roland Barthes" who argued "that it is impossible for a work of art to express a singular meaning. In other words, it is impossible to eliminate connotation, to prevent the uncontrolled proliferation of meanings attached to an object — there is no 'zero degree' of meaning in art."[20] Art is always *quasi parlando* — on the verge of saying something that it can never quite say. The interviewer goes on to add that "this is the major distinction between Prina and the so-called 'conceptual artists' working in the 1970s. Most conceptual artists tried to strip their art down to the point where it expressed only fundamental concepts. Prina himself may [focus] certain works on fairly abstract — one could even say conceptual — notions, but he also accepts and encourages the contamination of such concepts with historical, cultural and personal associations." The abstract, in other words, is never abstract; it is always situated historically. For Prina,

> the narrative of historical progress in art — which has been with us in one form or another at least since the Renaissance and which formed the backbone of the modernist movement — has been so thoroughly debunked by post-modern theory that it is simply no longer possible to talk about art developing in any logical way or progressing toward any general goal. But that's not all. At the same time that he thus denies art a general progressive purpose, Prina also closes off an avenue that has traditionally been viewed as one of

---

20 Julian M. Rose, "A Night and a Day with Stephen Prina," *The Harvard Crimson,* December 17, 2004, http://www.thecrimson.com/article/2004/12/17/a-night-and-a-day-with.

art's more specific purposes. This is personal expression, which he views as too cliché-ridden and problematic to be a viable artistic activity today. One might see these ideas as almost nihilistic, but in reality they are extraordinarily liberating. For what Prina has managed to do here is break down several deeply entrenched structures which in the past have dictated to the artist both how meaning should be made and what it should be (either meaning as personal expression or meaning as progress). Accordingly, he is left with a complete freedom in regard to meaning, an almost infinitely open field within which all meanings are possible and everything is potentially meaningful.[21]

Extended to Schoenberg, this suggests that his refusal of tonality constituted an artistic statement that went beyond musical composition, and maps on to a rejection of the idea of artistic progress, a position also held to vehemently by Gould. In this sense, Schoenberg's work can be understood as recursive in both the historical and formal senses — a turning back to a previous artistic era as well as the repeated application of a rule (as in his compositions with tone rows), a process that is now familiar to us through computation.[22]

Working in a similar vein to Prina is the avowedly post-Internet artist Cory Arcangel, who received his artistic training at the Oberlin Conservatory of Music as a classical guitar major.[23] Like Prina, he has produced work that takes as its *point de repère* musical compositions of Schoenberg and performances by Gould. His *A Couple Thousand Short Films About Glenn Gould* (2005) riffs on François Girard's 1993 *Thirty-Two Short Films About Glenn Gould*. Whereas Girard's film seeks to understand Gould's

---

21 Ibid..
22 The question of expression is more complicated in Schoenberg's case, though Rosen's book on Schoenberg suggests that atonality was a rejection of (or at least interrogation of) expressionism.
23 See Andrea K. Scott, "Futurism: Cory Arcangel Plays Around with Technology," *New Yorker,* May 30, 2011, https://www.newyorker.com/magazine/2011/05/30/futurism.

life via "snapshots" structured according to the 32 *Goldberg Variations* with which Gould's career had become identified, Arcangel pushes the boundary of this notion ontologically, splicing together circa 1100 clips of amateur musicians performing on YouTube.[24] The result is to expand the notion of music exponentially such that it no longer can be understood as a specialized activity (one that would be engaged in by professional musician in a dedicated place) but rather as an acoustic medium that now constitutes our environment. In the piece, "[e]ach note of the score jumps between individual clips of different musicians, with each screen carrying a separate melody line. The final effect is an almost hallucinatory montage — a flood of images. [...] Arcangel allows anonymous guitarists, keyboard players, tuba players and other enthusiasts from around the world to unintentionally collaborate in recreating Bach's masterpiece."[25] Art in this context is less a specialized practice than a mode of being.

Arcangel's *Drei Klavierstücke* (2009) uses a similar set of techniques to produce a performance of Schoenberg's piano composition of that name.[26] Splicing together YouTube videos of cats "playing" the piano, Arcangel reconfigured the notes to duplicate Schoenberg's three piano pieces as played by Gould. The work engages with Schoenberg on a number of levels by dethroning atonality as a specialized activity, thereby suggesting that the idea of "dissonance" is inherent in Internet culture,

---

24 Arcangel also published a book with the same title in 1106 unique copies (the number of clips that he spliced to produce his work): *A Couple Thousand Short Films About Glenn Gould* (Manchester: Cornerhouse, 2008).

25 "Cory Arcangel: 'a couple thousand short films about Glenn Gould,'" *Northern Gallery for Contemporary Art,* http://www.ngca.co.uk/exhibs/default.asp?id=117&prnt=18.

26 The work can be viewed on Arcangel's YouTube Channel: coryarcangel, "Cory Arcangel - Arnold Schoenberg, op. 11 - I - Cute Kittens," *YouTube,* July 6, 2009, https://www.youtube.com/watch?v=lF6IBWTDgnI; coryarcangel, "Cory Arcangel - Arnold Schoenberg, op. 11 - II - Cute Kittens," *YouTube,* July 6, 2009, https://www.youtube.com/watch?v=6ayonOIWS04; coryarcangel, "Cory Arcangel - Arnold Schoenberg, op. 11 - III - Cute Kittens," *YouTube,* July 6, 2009, https://www.youtube.com/watch?v=aHrMlgKrons.

which lacks a controlling center for the infinite strands of information by which it is formed. It also dethrones the idea of modernist art as a bulwark against kitsch, as Adorno had argued that it should be, thereby opening up the idea of classical art as extending beyond a strictly defined milieu, such as the concert hall. This reflects the democratization that Cage believed to be inherent in post-Schoenbergian music.

As acoustic works in galleries devoted to visual art, the works of Prina and Arcangel occupy a liminal space, and that space is paradigmatically the space of speechsong, which articulates a notion of artistic hybridity while also foreshadowing a postliterate understanding of artistic production. As speech that is not speech and song that is not song, speechsong occupies an acousmatic space that is congruent with the technologies of voice that now dominate the sonic landscape. Richard Taruskin states about his *Oxford History of Western Music* that

> its number-one postulate [is] that the literate tradition of Western music is coherent at least insofar as it has a completed shape. Its beginnings are known and explicable, and its end is now foreseeable (and also explicable). And just as the early chapters are dominated by the interplay of literate and preliterate modes of thinking and transmission (and the middle chapters try to cite enough examples to keep the interplay of literate and nonliterate alive in the reader's consciousness), so the concluding chapters are dominated by the interplay of literate and postliterate modes.[27]

---

27 See Richard Taruskin, "Introduction: The History of What?" to the *Oxford History of Western Music,* http://www.oxfordwesternmusic.com. Taruskin's comment that with literacy, music "could occupy space as well as time" fails to understand that sound is already spatial, a notion reflected in church architecture and the music created for it. It is this spatiality of sound that is a key component of Schoenberg's twelve tone compositions.

This overview of musical history is congruent with the media history traced by McLuhan in *The Gutenberg Galaxy*,[28] although McLuhan more accurately traces this history from oral to literate to *acoustic*, a "secondary orality" (in the formulation of Walter Ong), which has major implications for the understanding of music. If music is now entering a post-literate phase, as Taruskin suggests, a phase in which acoustic space prevails, that shift was articulated by Schoenberg in his rejection of the linear and teleological aspects of music inherited from literacy (exemplified by Wagner's *Handlung*), and is evident in Gould's technological performance practices of the splice and of multiple takes. It is this shift to acoustic space that *Moses und Aron* adumbrates. The site of mediatic translation from song to speech and speech to song, *Sprechstimme* embodies the recursions of media history and does so as a mode of practice.

---

28 Marshall McLuhan, *The Gutenberg Galaxy: The Making of Typographic Man* (Toronto: University of Toronto Press, 1962).

Bibliography

Adams, Kyle. "The Musical Analysis of Hip-Hop." In *The Cambridge Companion to Hip-Hop,* edited by Justin A. Williams, 118–34. Cambridge: Cambridge University Press, 2015.

Adorno, Theodor W., and Max Horkheimer. "The Culture Industry." In *Dialectic of Enlightenment,* translated by Edmund Jephcott, 94–136. Stanford: Stanford University Press, 2002.

———. *Philosophy of New Music.* Translated, edited, and with an introduction by Robert Hullot-Kenter. Minneapolis: University of Minnesota Press, 2004.

———. *Prisms.* Translated by Samuel and Sherry Weber. Cambridge: MIT Press, 1967.

———. "Sacred Fragment." In *Quasi una fantasia,* translated by Rodney Livingstone, 225–48. London: Verso, 1992.

Agamben, Giorgio. *The Coming Community.* Translated by Michael Hardt. Minneapolis: University of Minnesota Press, 1993.

Arcangel, Cory. *A Couple Thousand Short Films About Glenn Gould.* Manchester: Cornerhouse, 2008.

Arved, Ashby. "Schoenberg, Boulez, and Twelve-Tone Composition as 'Ideal Type.'" *Journal of the American*

Musicological Society 54, no. 3 (2001): 585–625. DOI: 10.1525/jams.2001.54.3.585.

Ashton, Dore. *A Fable of Modern Art*. London: Thames & Hudson, 1980.

Auner, Joseph. "Composing on Stage: Schoenberg and the Creative Process as Public Performance." *19th Century Music* 29, no. 1 (2005): 64–93. DOI: 10.1525/ncm.2005.29.1.64.

———, ed. *A Schoenberg Reader: Documents of a Life*. New Haven: Yale University Press, 2003.

Bahr, Erhard. *Weimar on the Pacific: German Exile Culture in Los Angeles and the Crisis of Modernism*. Berkeley: University of California Press, 2007.

Bailey, Kathryn. "Webern's Row Tables." In *Webern Studies*, edited by Kathryn Bailey, 170–228. Cambridge: Cambridge University Press, 1996.

Barthes, Roland. "Rasch." In *The Responsibility of Forms: Critical Essays on Music, Art and Representation*, translated by Richard Howard, 299–312. New York: Hill and Wang, 1985.

Bazzana, Kevin. *Glenn Gould: The Performer in the Work*. Oxford: Clarendon Press, 1997.

———. *Wondrous Strange: The Life and Art of Glenn Gould*. Toronto: McClelland and Stewart, 2003.

Beckwith, John. *In Search of Alberto Guerrero*. Waterloo: Wilfrid Laurier University Press, 2006.

Biswas, Allie. "Stephen Prina." *Studio International*, May 17, 2016. http://www.studiointernational.com/index.php/stephen-prina-interview-galesburg-illinois.

Bø-Rygg, Arnfinn. "The Finished Fragment: On Arnold Schoenberg's *Moses und Aron*." In *Transcendence and Sensoriness: Perceptions, Revelation, and the Arts,* edited by Svein Aage Christofferson et al., 249–86. Leiden: Brill, 2015.

Boulez, Pierre. "Schoenberg Is Dead." In *Notes of an Apprenticeship,* translated by Herbert Weinstock, 268–75. New York: Random House, 1968.

Brand, Juliane, and Christopher Hailey, eds. *Creative Dissonance: Arnold Schoenberg and the Transformations of Twentieth-Century Culture*. Berkeley: University of California Press, 1997.

Brown, Julie. *Schoenberg and Redemption*. Cambridge: Cambridge University Press, 2014.

———. "Schoenberg's Early Wagnerisms: Atonality and the Redemption of Ahasuerus." *Cambridge Opera Journal* 6, no. 1 (1994): 51–80. DOI: 10.1017/S0954586700004134.

Bujić, Bojan. *Arnold Schoenberg*. London: Phaidon, 2011.

Busoni, Ferruccio. *Sketch of a New Aesthetic of Music*. Translated by T. Baker. New York: Schirmer, 1911.

Cage, John. "Credo." In *Sound by Artists*, edited by Dan Lander and Micah Lexier, 15–19. Toronto: Art Metropole, 1990.

Cahn. Steven J. "Review of *Schoenberg and Redemption*, by Julie Brown." *Music and Letters* 97, no. 4 (2016): 665–67. DOI: 10.1093/ml/gcw066.

Kaliss, Jeff. "Praising Uri Caine." *San Francisco Classical Voice*, June 4, 2014. https://www.sfcv.org/events-calendar/artist-spotlight/praising-uri-caine.

Cavell, Richard. *McLuhan in Space: A Cultural Geography*. Toronto: University of Toronto Press, 2002.

———. *Remediating McLuhan*. Amsterdam: Amsterdam University Press, 2016.

Cherlin, Michael. "Schoenberg's Music for the Theater." In *The Great Tradition and its Legacy: The Evolution of Dramatic and Musical Theater in Austria and Central Europe*, edited by Michael Cherlin et al., 246–58. New York: Berghahn, 2004.

Cornell, Lauren, and Ed Halter, eds. *Mass Effect: Art and the Internet in the Twenty-First Century*. Cambridge: MIT Press, 2015.

coryarcangel. "Cory Arcangel - Arnold Schoenberg, op. 11 - I - Cute Kittens." *YouTube*, July 6, 2009. https://www.youtube.com/watch?v=lF6IBWTDgnI.

———. "Cory Arcangel - Arnold Schoenberg, op. 11 - II - Cute Kittens." *YouTube*, July 6, 2009. https://www.youtube.com/watch?v=6ayonOIWSo4.

———. "Cory Arcangel - Arnold Schoenberg, op. 11 - III - Cute Kittens." *YouTube,* July 6, 2009. https://www.youtube.com/watch?v=aHrMlgKrons.

"Cory Arcangel: 'a couple thousand short films about Glenn Gould.'" *Northern Gallery for Contemporary Art.* http://www.ngca.co.uk/exhibs/default.asp?id=117&prnt=18.

Cott, Jonathan. *Conversations with Glenn Gould.* Boston: Little Brown, 1984.

Coupland, Douglas. *Marshall McLuhan.* Toronto: Penguin, 2009.

Covach, John. "Schoenberg's 'Poetics of Music,' the Twelve-Tone Method, and the Musical Idea." In *Schoenberg and Words: The Modernist Years,* edited by Charlotte M. Cross and Russell A. Berman, 309–46. New York: Garland, 2000.

Critchley, Simon. "Being and Time part 4: Thrown into this World." *The Guardian,* June 29, 2009. http://www.theguardian.com/commentisfree/belief/2009/jun/29/religion-philosophy.

Dante Alighieri, *La divina commedia,* ed. Giorgio Petrocchi. Turin: Einaudi, 1975.

Darack, Arthur. "Foreword" to Glenn Gould, *Arnold Schoenberg: A Perspective,* v–viii. Cincinnati: University of Cincinnati Press, 1964.

Dolar, Mladen. *A Voice and Nothing More.* Cambridge: MIT Press, 2006.

Dyson, Frances. "The Ear That Would Hear Sounds In Themselves: John Cage 1945–1965." In *Wireless Imagination: Sound, Radio and the Avant-Garde,* edited by Douglas Kahn and Gregory Whitehead, 373–401. Cambridge: MIT Press, 1992.

Eichler, Dominic. "Point Counter Point." *Frieze,* May 5, 2009. https://frieze.com/article/point-counter-point.

Eisler, Hanns. *Brecht, Music and Culture: Hanns Eisler in Conversation with Hans Bunge.* London: Bloomsbury, 2014.

Eliot, T.S. "Tradition and the Individual Talent." *The Egoist,* September and November, 1919. http://tseliot.com/essays/tradition-and-the-individual-talent.

Feisst, Sabine. *Schoenberg's New World: The American Years*. Oxford: Oxford University Press, 2011.
Friedrich, Otto. *Glenn Gould: A Life and Variations*. Toronto: Lester and Orpen Dennys, 1989.
Goethe, Johann Wolfgang von. *Conversations with Eckerman*. Translated by Margaret Fuller. London: Hilliard, Gray, 1839.
Gould, Glenn. *Arnold Schoenberg: A Perspective*. Cincinnati: University of Cincinnati Press, 1964.
———. *La série Schoenberg*. Edited by Ghyslaine Guertin. Paris: Christian Bourgois, 1998.
———. *The Glenn Gould Reader*. Edited by Tim Page. Toronto: Lester & Orpen Dennys, 1984.
Grant, Colin. "The Theatre Where It Happens." *The Times Literary Supplement,* January 12, 2018. https://www.the-tls.co.uk/articles/public/the-theatre-where-it-happens/.
HaCohen, Ruth. "Arnold Schoenberg: Sonic Allegories." In *Makers of Jewish Modernity,* edited by Jacques Picard et al., 173–86. Princeton: Princeton University Press, 2016.
———. *The Music Libel against the Jews*. New Haven: Yale University Press, 2011.
Hahl-Koch, Jelena, ed. *Arnold Schoenberg / Wassily Kandinsky: Letters, Pictures and Documents*. Translated by John C. Crawford. London: Faber, 1984.
Hanssen, Beatrice. "Dissonance and Aesthetic Totality: Adorno Reads Schönberg." In *Sound Figures of Modernity: German Music and Philosophy,* edited by Jost Hermand and Gerhard Richter, 181–200. Madison: University of Wisconsin Press, 2006.
Hines, Thomas S. "'Then Not Yet "Cage"': The Los Angeles Years, 1912–1938." In *John Cage: Composed in America,* edited by Marjorie Perloff and Charles Junkerman, 65–99. Chicago: University of Chicago Press, 1994.
Holl, Ute. *The Moses Complex: Freud, Schoenberg, Straub/Huillet*. Translated by Michael Turnbull. Zurich & Berlin: Diaphanes, 2017.
Innis, Harold Adams. *Empire and Communications*. Oxford: Clarendon Press, 1950.

Jayne, Edward. "Metaphoric Hypersignification, Metonymic Designification." *Centennial Review* 38, no. 1 (1994): 9–32. https://www.jstor.org/stable/23739678.

Johnson, Julian. "Schoenberg, Modernism and Metaphysics." In *The Cambridge Companion to Schoenberg*, edited by Jennifer Shaw and Joseph Auner, 108–19. Cambridge: Cambridge University Press, 2010.

Kane, Brian. *Sound Unseen: Acousmatic Sound in Theory and Practice*. Oxford: Oxford University Press, 2016.

Kennedy, Michael, and Joyce Bourne, eds. *Concise Oxford Dictionary of Music*. Oxford: Oxford University Press, 2007.

Kingwell, Mark. *Glenn Gould*. Toronto: Penguin, 2009.

Kittler, Friedrich. *Gramophone Film Typewriter*. Translated by Geoffrey Winthrop-Young and Michael Wutz. Stanford: Stanford University Press, 1999.

———. "Pathos and Ethos: An Aristotelian Observation." In *The Truth of the Technological World*, edited by Hans Ulrich Gumbrecht, 303–6. Stanford: Stanford University Press, 2013.

———."The God of the Ears." In *The Truth of the Technological World*, edited by Hans Ulrich Gumbrecht, 45–56. Stanford: Stanford University Press, 2013.

———. "World-Breath: On Wagner's Media Technology." In *Opera through Other Eyes*, edited by David J. Levin, 215–35. Stanford: Stanford University Press, 1994.

Kurth, Richard. "Immanence and Transcendence in *Moses und Aron*." In *The Cambridge Companion to Schoenberg*, edited by Jennifer Shaw and Joseph Auner, 177–90. Cambridge: Cambridge University Press, 2011.

Lacan, Jacques. *Écrits: A Selection*. Translated by Alan Sheridan. London: Tavistock, 1977.

Leibowitz, René. *Schoenberg and His School: The Contemporary State of the Language of Music*. Translated by Dika Newlin. New York: Da Capo, 1949.

Leroux, George. *Partita for Glenn Gould*. Translated by Donald Winkler. Montreal: McGill-Queens University Press, 2010.

Llano, Pedro de. "Displacement and Translation in the Work of Stephen Prina." *Afterall,* September 7, 2009. https://afterall.org/online/displacement.and.translation.in.the.work.of.stephen.prina.

Macmillan, Ernest. *Macmillan on Music: Essays by Sir Ernest Macmillan.* Toronto: Dundurn Press, 1997.

Maloney, S. Timothy. "Glenn Gould, Autistic Savant." In *Sounding Off: Theorizing Disability in Music,* edited by Neil Lerner and Joseph Straus, 121–36. New York: Routledge, 2006.

Marcus, Kenneth H. *Schoenberg and Hollywood Modernism.* Cambridge: Cambridge University Press, 2015.

Martin, Benjamin G. *The Nazi-Fascist New Order for European Culture.* Cambridge: Harvard University Press, 2017.

McLuhan, Marshall. "Canada: The Borderline Case." In *The Canadian Imagination,* edited by David Staines, 226–48. Cambridge: Harvard University Press, 1977.

———. *The Gutenberg Galaxy: The Making of Typographic Man.* Toronto: University of Toronto Press, 1962.

———. The *Mechanical Bride: Folklore of Industrial Man.* New York: Vanguard Press, 1951.

———. *Understanding Media: The Extensions of Man.* New York: McGraw-Hill, 1964.

———, and Quentin Fiore. *The Medium is the Massage: An Inventory of Effects.* New York: Random House, 1967.

———, and Eric McLuhan. *Laws of Media: The New Science.* Toronto: University of Toronto Press, 1988.

———, and Barrington Nevitt. *Take Today: The Executive as Dropout.* Toronto: Longman, 1972.

Menuhin, Yehudi. *Unfinished Journey.* New York: Knopf, 1997.

Motte-Haber, Helga de la. "Space–Environment–Shared World: Robin Minard's Sound Installations." In *Robin Minard: Silent Music/Between Sound Art and Acoustic Design,* edited by B. Schulz, 34–56. Heidelberg: Kehrer, 1999.

Nielinger-Vakil, Carola. *Luigi Nono: A Composer in Context.* Cambridge: Cambridge University Press, 2015.

Nietzsche, Friedrich. *Die Geburt der Tragödie.* Leipzig: Fritzsch, 1878. http://www.nietzschesource.org/#eKGWB/GT.

———. *The Birth of Tragedy out of the Spirit of Music.* Translated by Douglas Smith. Oxford: Oxford University Press, 2000.

Noudelmann, François. *The Philosopher's Touch: Sartre, Nietzsche and Barthes at the Piano.* Translated by Brian J. Reilly. Columbia: Columbia University Press, 2012.

Oestreich, James R. "Review: Works with Hélène Grimaud, Daniel Barenboim and Others." *New York Times,* May 6, 2016. https://www.nytimes.com/2016/05/07/arts/music/review-works-by-helene-grimaud-daniel-barenboim-and-others.html.

Ong, Walter. *Orality and Literacy: The Technologizing of the Word.* New York: Methuen, 1982.

Orr, David, and Dinitia Smith. "Pulitzer-Winning Poetic Voice Often Echoed, Never Matched." *New York Times,* September 4, 2017: A1, A16.

Ostwald, Peter. *Glenn Gould: The Ecstasy and Tragedy of Genius.* New York: Norton, 1998.

Ouzounian, Gascia. "Sound Installation Art." In *Music, Sound and Space: Transformations of Public and Private Experience,* 73–89. Cambridge: Cambridge University Press, 2013.

Payzant, Geoffrey. *Glenn Gould: Music and Mind.* Toronto: Van Nostrand Reinhold, 1978.

Peters, John Durham. "The Ten Commandments as Media Theory." In *Communication and Social Life: Studies in Honor of Professor Esteban López-Escobar,* edited by Maxwell McCombs and Manuel Martín Algarra, 275–84. Pamplona: Ediciones Universidad de Navarra, 2012.

Pettman, Dominic. *Sonic Intimacy: Voice, Species, Technics.* Stanford: Stanford University Press, 2017.

Philipse, Herman. *Heidegger's Philosophy of Being: A Critical Interpretation.* Princeton: Princeton University Press, 2001.

Pound, Ezra. "Vorticism." *Fortnightly Review* 96 n.s., September 1, 1914. http://fortnightlyreview.co.uk/vorticism/.

Powe, Bruce W. "A Search for Glenn Gould." In *The Solitary Outlaw*, 135–65. Toronto: Lester & Orpen Dennys, 1987.
Rebstock, Matthias. "Composed Theatre: Mapping the Field." In *Composed Theatre: Aesthetics, Practices, Processes*, edited by Rebstock and David Roesner, 17–52. Bristol: Intellect, 2012.
Rehding, Alexander. "Introduction: Discrete/Continuous: Music and Media Theory after Kittler: A Colloquy." *Journal of the American Musicological Society* 70, no. 1 (2017): 221–27. DOI: 10.1525/jams.2017.70.1.221.
———. "Moses's Beginning." *Opera Quarterly* 2, no. 4 (2007): 395–417. DOI: 10.1093/oq/kbn036.
Ringer, Alexander R. *Arnold Schoenberg: The Composer as Jew.* Oxford: Clarendon Press, 1990.
Roberts, John P.L., ed. *The Art of Glenn Gould.* Toronto: Malcolm Lester Books, 1999.
———. "Preface I." In *Glenn Gould: Selected Letters*, edited by Roberts and Ghyslaine Guertin, vii–xvi. Toronto: Oxford University Press, 1992.
——— and Ghyslaine Guertin, eds. *Glenn Gould: Selected Letters.* Toronto: Oxford University Press, 1992.
Roddy, Joseph. "Apollonian." *New Yorker,* May 14, 1960, 51–93.
Roesner, David. "Introduction: Composed Theatre in Context." In *Composed Theatre: Aesthetics, Practices, Processes*, edited by Matthias Rebstock and Roesner, 10–14. Bristol: Intellect, 2012.
Rose, Julian M. "A Night and a Day with Stephen Prina." *The Harvard Crimson,* December 17, 2004. http://www.thecrimson.com/article/2004/12/17/a-night-and-a-day-with.
Rosen, Charles. *Schoenberg.* London: Fontana, 1976.
Russolo, Luigi. *L'arte dei rumori.* Milan: Edizioni Futuriste, 1916.
Sadie, Stanley, ed. *The New Grove Dictionary of Music and Musicians.* London: Macmillan, 2001.
Said, Edward. "The Music Itself: Glenn Gould's Contrapuntal Vision." In *Glenn Gould: Variations,* ed. John McGreevy, 45–54. Toronto: Doubleday, 1983.

Sanden, Michael. *Liveness in Modern Music*. New York: Routledge, 2012.

Sanderson, Blair. "Review of 'Glenn Gould, The Acoustic Orchestrations – Scriabin and Sibelius.'" *AllMusic*. https://www.allmusic.com/album/glenn-gould-the-acoustic-orchestrations-works-by-scriabin-and-sibelius-mw0002428189.

Saul, John Ralston. "Canada 160 Years Later." *Globe and Mail*, March 11, 2008. https://www.theglobeandmail.com/opinion/canada-160-years-later/article718521/.

Schaeffer, Pierre. "Acousmatics." In *Audio Culture: Readings in Modern Music*, 76–81. New York: Continuum, 2004.

Schafer, R. Murray. *The Tuning of the World*. New York: Knopf, 1977.

Schneider, Michel. *Glenn Gould Piano Solo*. Paris: Gallimard, 1988.

Schoenberg, Arnold. *Arnold Schoenberg Letters*. Edited by Erwin Stein. Translated by Eithne Wilkins and Ernst Kaiser. New York: St. Martin's Press, 1965.

———. "Breslau lecture on *Die glückliche Hand*." In *Arnold Schoenberg / Wassily Kandinsky: Letters, Pictures and Documents*. Edited by Jelena Hahl-Koch, translated by John C. Crawford, 102–7. London: Faber and Faber, 1984.

———. *Schoenberg's "Moses and Aaron."* Edited by Karl H. Worner. Translated by Paul Hamburger. London: Faber and Faber, 1963.

———. *Style and Idea: Selected Writings*. Edited by Leonard Stein and translated by Leo Black. Berkeley: University of California Press 1984.

———. *Theory of Harmony*. Translated by Roy Carter. Berkeley: University of California Press, 1978.

Schorske, Carl. *Fin-de-Siècle Vienna: Politics and Culture*. New York: Knopf, 1980.

Scott, Andrea K. "Futurism: Cory Arcangel Plays Around with Technology." *New Yorker*, May 30, 2011. https://www.newyorker.com/magazine/2011/05/30/futurism.

Sealey, Mark. "Review of *Theory of Harmony.*" *Classical Net*, 2010. http://www.classical.net/music/books/reviews/0520266080a.php.

Shanno, Lucy. "Composing with Recording in Mind: An Analytic Approach." PhD dissertation, University of Pennsylvania, 2007. https://repository.upenn.edu/dissertations/AAI3271813.

Shawn, Allen. *Arnold Schoenberg's Journey.* New York: Farrar, Straus & Giroux, 2002.

Shoaf, R. Wayne, and Susan L. Sloan. *Schoenberg's Dodecaphonic Devices.* Exhibition catalog. Los Angeles: Arnold Schoenberg Institute, 1989.

Slavet, Eliza. "A Matter of Distinction: On Recent Work by Jan Assmann." *AJS Review* 34, no. 2 (2010): 385–93. DOI: 10.1017/S0364009410000656.

Smith, Bruce R. *The Acoustic World of Early Modern England: Attending to the O-Factor.* Chicago: University of Chicago Press, 1999.

Stillman, Steel. "In The Studio: Stephen Prina." *Art in America,* April 26, 2013. http://www.artinamericamagazine.com/news-features/magazines/in-the-studio-stephen-prina.

Stuckenschmidt, H.H. *Schoenberg: His Life, World, and Work.* Translated by Humphrey Searle. London: Calder, 1977.

Taruskin, Richard. *The Oxford History of Western Music.* Oxford: Oxford University Press, 2009. http://www.oxfordwesternmusic.com.

———. "The Poietic Fallacy." *Musical Times* 145 (2004): 7–34. DOI: 10.2307/4149092.

Tomlinson, Gary. "Musicology, Anthropology, History." In *The Cultural Study of Music,* edited by Martin Clayton et al., 31–44. New York: Routledge, 2003.

Tommasini, Anthony. "Glenn Gould's Treasures for the Taking." *New York Times,* February 4, 2018, AR, 8.

Wagner, Richard. *Das Judenthum in der Musik.* Leipzig: Weber, 1869. https://de.wikisource.org/wiki/Das_Judenthum_in_der_Musik_(1869).

———. *The Jew in Music.* Translated by William Ashton Ellis. London: Kegan Paul, 1894. http://www.jrbooksonline.com/pdf_books/judaisminmusic.pdf.

———. *Tristan und Isolde: Handlung in drei Aufzügen.* Frankfurt: Insel, 2000.

Werner, Erich. *The Sacred Bridge: Liturgical Parallels in Synagogue and Early Church.* London: Dobson, 1959.

Winter, Franz. "Gustave Mahler (1860–1911)." Liner notes, Gustav Mahler/Uri Caine, *Urlicht/Primal Light.* Winter & Winter 910 004-2, 1997, compact disc.

Wörner, Karl H. *Schoenberg's "Moses and Aaron."* Translated by Paul Hamburger. London: Faber and Faber, 1963.

Wright, James, K., and Alan M. Gillmor, eds. *Schoenberg's Chamber Music, Schoenberg's World.* Hillsdale: Pendragon Press, 2009.

Discography

Gould, Glenn. *The Acoustic Orchestrations: Works by Scriabin and Sibelius.* Recorded July 16–17, 1970, Sony Classical 887254065722, 2012, compact disc.

———. *Glenn Gould's Solitude Trilogy: Three Sound Documentaries.* Canadian Broadcasting Corporation PSCD 2003-3, 1992, 3 compact discs.

Harrison, Lou. "Three Coyote Stories." *Lou Harrison: A Portrait.* Barry Jekowsky and Al Jarreau and California Symphony Orchestra. Recorded October 17, 1997. Decca B01FNDE7MU, 2016, 1 compact disc.

Ieki, Yoshiko, harpsichordist. *Bach: Goldberg Variations BWV 988.* Recorded June 15, 2018. Regulus, 2018, 2 compact discs.

Mahler, Gustave/Uri Caine. *Urlicht/Primal Light.* Winter & Winter 910 004-2, 1997, compact disc.

www.ingramcontent.com/pod-product-compliance
Lightning Source LLC
Chambersburg PA
CBHW051130160426
43195CB00014B/2414